Peckover House,
Cambridgeshire

C

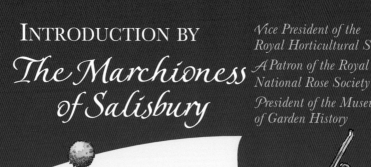

INTRODUCTION BY
The Marchioness of Salisbury

Vice President of the Royal Horticultural Society

A Patron of the Royal National Rose Society

President of the Museum of Garden History

I am delighted to welcome readers of this guide to a corner of England, which from a gardener's viewpoint is a very special one, with many notable gardens for you to visit and enjoy. You will find a wide choice, and whether you admire the small and intimate, the large landscape or the intricacies of the classical parterre, not to speak of the fantasies of the Tudor & Jacobean gardens, I do not doubt that you will find a garden in this region to give you the pleasures you are seeking.

Amongst them is the garden at Hatfield House in Hertfordshire that was created by my husband, Lord Salisbury's, ancestor Robert Cecil between 1607 and 1611. He employed Salaman de Caux, the Dutchman (as he is described at that time) to design his garden and John Tradescant, the famous gardener and plant hunter to plant it, sending him abroad to find new plants for Hatfield. I came to live at Hatfield after my father-in-law's death in 1972, and so for 28 years have planned and planted the gardens here. There was much to be done to restore, and to try and improve them.

It's my great good fortune to have a special love for gardens of the Tudor and Stuart times and so to indulge this love in the gardens here. It was a delight to design and plant a knot garden for the Tudor Palace, which is within the grounds, and to collect historical plants for it, such as the old roses which were grown at that time, and which Queen Elizabeth I must have known as a young Princess when she was a virtual prisoner in the Palace, as well as a collection of historical tulips and narcissus, which were given to me by the Hortus Bulborum in Holland. My great love is for the old fashioned flowers such as the Pinks and Poppies, ancient Roses, Auriculas, Pansies and Violas, and you will see them in abundance at Hatfield. Each season presents something of beauty and interest, and it is impossible to choose a favourite one. Even in the cold of February, there are the sheets of snowdrops in the Spring wood beyond the New Pond, and we open for them to be viewed on "Snowdrop Sundays". While in November the autumn colours can be seen at their most spectacular.

Hatfield House Garden, Hertfordshire

Of course, Hatfield is just one of the many remarkable and beautiful gardens to be discovered in the East of England, and I hope that you will enjoy reading this guide to them, and that your reading will lead to some wonderful days spent visiting *The Gardens of the East of England*

5

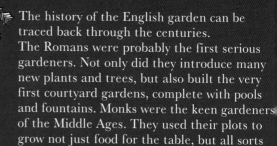

A POTTED HISTORY

of the English Garden

The history of the English garden can be traced back through the centuries.

The Romans were probably the first serious gardeners. Not only did they introduce many new plants and trees, but also built the very first courtyard gardens, complete with pools and fountains. Monks were the keen gardeners of the Middle Ages. They used their plots to grow not just food for the table, but all sorts of herbs for medicine, too.

The pomp and circumstance of the Tudor period was a great time in the history of gardens. Spectacular stately homes needed magnificent parks and ornate gardens. All sorts of fancies were introduced like sundials, knot gardens and hedge mazes and exotic new species were introduced from voyages to far away places. Perhaps even more important, the first plant books were published and botany became a recognised science.

17th century gardens became even more cosmopolitan with a strong French and Dutch influence. From France came the 'parterre', one large garden spilt into different areas, while avenues of trees marched in strict straight lines across the adjacent parkland. From 1688, Dutch ideas were all the rage with dramatic water features, bulbs and topiary. Come the 18th century and the tidy look of the French and Dutch gardens were replaced by more informal designs. Now, the once separate parkland was incorporated into the more traditional garden using temples, obelisks and other architectural features as eye-catching points. From this period came one of Britain's greatest garden designers, Lancelot "Capability" Brown. His designs incorporated three natural ingredients, water, trees and terrain.

Engine House, Cambridgeshire

Far Right- Belton House, Lincolnshire

The next great designer, Humphry Repton, reduced the vast parkland and brought a more traditional garden back to the confines of the house. Towards the end of his life, the fashion for flower gardens was blooming again. The Victorians loved them too, and continued the trend. They favoured vast displays of plants and flowers plus all sorts of traditional features – statuary, fountains, greenhouses and twee little thatched buildings. In our cities and towns, public parks were opened, while the many tree species collected from abroad, led to the development of the Arboretum.

In the 1870's, the Irishman, William Robinson, developed the idea of wild or natural gardens with the emphasis on the plant as the basis of the garden rather than the design.

Two distinct types of garden were popular at the start of the 20th century:- Robinson's 'plantsmans' or wild garden, alongside the more traditional formal garden.

One of the most well-known figures of the time was Gertrude Jekyll, regarded as the founder of modern gardening. She is particularly associated with the development of the herbaceous border, an idea which probably came from the traditional cottage gardens dating from the 16th and 17th centuries. Today, the informal style rules with little interest in the formal grand gardens of yesteryear.

Spilsby, Lincolnshire

Exploring the gardens of the Real England can be a fascinating tour through history as well as a delight for the senses. But, as Kipling put it,

"The Glory of the Garden lies in more than meets the eye."

7

Throughout the year, the East of England is home to a wonderful selection of garden-related events – from a carnival parade of floats decorated with thousands of tulip heads, to traditional country shows and fetes with their gardening competitions. Enjoy the spectacular displays at our flower festivals or be a real 'nosey parker' and explore the secret gardens of our picturesque villages at numerous open days. Over the next few pages we have brought together information on a selection of garden events taking place during 2000. Some of the events are still provisional at the time this guide was put together and these are indicated by an *.

Gardens of the Rose, Hertfordshire

PRIVATE GARDENS OPEN

Alongside these events, there will be many other private gardens (large and small) opening their doors to the public, in aid of numerous charities. The following produce free leaflets highlighting the gardens open in their relevant counties during the year. The owners of these gardens donate all or most of the proceeds to the charity concerned.
British Red Cross – Beds (01234) 349166, Cambs (01223) 354434, Essex (01245) 490090, Herts (01992) 586609, Lincs (01476) 563378, Norfolk (01603) 426361, Suffolk (01284) 767215
St. John's Ambulance – Cambs (01223) 355334, Essex (01245) 265678, Lincs (01522) 523701, Norfolk (01603) 621649, Suffolk (01473) 241500
Lincolnshire Old Churches Trust (01507) 603918
Suffolk Historic Churches Trust (01787) 883884

THE NATIONAL GARDENS SCHEME

For over 70 years, the National Gardens Scheme has been raising money for many deserving causes by the opening of private gardens, the majority of which are not normally open to the public. In 1998, over £1.4 million was raised through the scheme for beneficiaries such as The Queen's Nursing Institute (for the welfare of elderly and needy district nurses), The Gardens Fund of the National Trust (and for the education and training of gardeners through NGS bursaries), and for the Macmillan Cancer Relief. Each year, an excellent guide is produced listing the gardens open during the year. This is available from bookshops at £4.50, or from the National Gardens Scheme, Hatchlands Park, East Clandon, Guildford, Surrey GU4 7RT (priced at £5.75 including post and package).

1 Jan -31 Dec

Millennium Orchard
Museum of St Albans, Hatfield

End Jan/Feb

Snowdrop Walks
Walsingham Abbey Grounds, Walsingham, Norfolk

3-6 Feb*

Springfields Horticultural Exhibition
Springfields Exhibition Centre, Camelgate, Spalding, Lincs

5-6 Feb

Winter Bonsai Show
Capel Manor Gardens, Bullsmoor Lane, Enfield, Middlesex

13 Feb

Snowdrops Open Day
Kings Arms Path Garden, Kings Arms Yard, Ampthill, Beds

18-20, 24-26 Feb

Clematis Pruning Demonstrations Thorncroft Clematis
Nursery, The Lings, Reymerston, Norfolk

20, 27 Feb, &
all Suns in Mar, Apr

Spring Garden Days *(for bulb displays)*, Doddington Hall &
Gardens, Doddington, Lincs

End Feb-early Mar

Snowdrop Open Days Benington Lordship Gardens,
Benington, nr. Stevenage, Herts

End Feb-early Mar

Snowdrop Weekends Hedingham Castle,
Castle Hedingham, nr. Halstead, Essex

4-5 Mar

Winter Open Weekend
Bressingham Gardens, Bressingham, nr Diss, Norfolk

13 Mar-7 May

World of Flowers
Springfields Show Gardens, Camelgate, Spalding, Lincs

26 Mar*

Chippenham Park Open Gardens
Chippenham, nr. Newmarket, Cambs

Early Apr

Primrose Week Alby Crafts & Gardens,
Erpingham, Norfolk

7 Apr-25 May*

Art of the Garden Exhibition
Cressing Temple, Witham, Essex

9

GARDEN EVENTS

7-9 Apr *	**Capel Manor Spring & Country Show** Capel Manor Gardens, Bullsmoor Lane, Enfield, Middlesex
8-9 Apr	**32nd Thriplow Daffodil Weekend** Thriplow, Cambs
8-9 Apr	**West Norfolk Spring Plant Fair** Avenue Road, Hunstanton, Norfolk
15-16 Apr	**Cambridgeshire Spring Garden & Interiors Show** Huntingdon Racecourse, Cambs
15-16 Apr	**Wood Sale and Fair** Ickworth House, Park & Gardens, Horringer, Suffolk
16-30 Apr	**Primrose Weeks** Fairhaven Woodlands & Water Gardens, School Road, South Walsham, Norfolk
21-24 Apr	**Country Skills and Working Craft Fair** Blickling Hall, Park and Gardens, Blickling, Norfolk
23-24 Apr	**Daffodil Day** Elsham Hall & Wildlife Park, Brigg, Lincs
23-24 Apr	**Garden Show** Elton Hall, Elton, Cambs
23 Apr	**Little Easton Manor Gardens** *(open in aid of SSAFFA)* Little Easton, nr. Dunmow, Essex
24 Apr	**Lathyrus Spring Open Day** Weavers Cottage, 35 Streetly End, West Wickham, Cambs
26 Apr	**Belton Garden Tour** Belton House, Park and Gardens, Belton, nr. Grantham, Lincs
26 Apr-7 May *	**South Holland Church Flower Festivals** Various churches throughout South Holland District, Lincs
29 Apr-1 May	**Spalding Flower Festival & Springfields Country Fair** *(parade on 29th)* Town Centre & Springfields, Camelgate, Spalding, Lincs
29 Apr-1 May	**Spring Garden Festival** Audley End House & Gardens, Essex
30 Apr-7 May	**Bluebell Open Days** Haughley Park, Haughley, nr. Stowmarket, Suffolk
30 Apr	**Mannington Gardens Open Day** *(for National Gardens Scheme)*, Mannington Hall, Norwich, Norfolk
30 Apr	**Moulton Chapel Flower Parade** Moulton Chapel, nr. Spalding, Lincs

GARDEN EVENTS

7 May	**N.C.C.P.G. Plant Sale** Marks Hall Estate & Arboretum, Coggeshall, Essex
13-14 May	**Knebworth Garden Show** Knebworth House, Gardens & Park, Knebworth, nr. Stevenage, Herts
13-14 May	**Norfolk Spring Garden and Interiors Show** Fakenham Racecourse, Cambs
14-31 May	**Candelabra Primula Weeks** Fairhaven Woodlands and Water Gardens, School Road, South Walsham, Norfolk
14 May	**Plant Fair** Elgood's Brewery Gardens, North Brink, Cambs
14 May	**Plant Fair and Plant Sale** Wimpole Hall, Arrington, Hertfordshire
14 May	**Swiss Garden Open Day** Old Warden, Beds
19-21 May	**Spring Garden & Craft Weekend** The Gardens of the Rose, Chiswell Green, nr. St. Albans, Herts
21 May	**The Beale Arboretum Open Day** West Lodge Park, Hadley Wood, nr. Barnet, Herts
21 May	**Garden Open** The Priory, Stoke-by-Nayland, Suffolk
21 May	**Hall Farm Garden Open Day** *(for Lincolnshire Old Churches Trust)*, Harpswell, Gainsborough, Lincs
21 May	**Plant Sale** Euston Hall and Garden, Euston, Norfolk
27-29 May	**Flower Festival** St. Andrew's Church, Church Road, Wormingford, Essex
27-29 May	**Garden Fair** Wrest Park Gardens, Silsoe, Beds
27-28 May	**Hertfordshire County Show** Hertfordshire County Showground, Dunstable Road, Redbourn, Herts
28 May	**Bury in Bloom Spring Flower Market** Bury St Edmunds, Suffolk
28-29 May	**Cotton Village Gardens Open** Cotton, Suffolk
28-29 May	**Gardens of Langham** nr Colchester, Essex
28 May	**Open Gardens & Plant Sale** 6 North Lane, Navenby, Lincs
29 May	**Woodhall Spa Agricultural Show** Jubilee Park, Stixwould Road, Woodhall Spa Lincs
31 May - 3 Jun	**Suffolk Show** Suffolk Showground, Bucklesham Road, Ipswich, Suffolk

GARDEN EVENTS

Early Jun	**Orchid Week** Alby Crafts & Gardens, Erpingham, Norfolk
Throughout Jun, Jul & Aug	**The Gardens of the Rose 'Summer Season 2000'** Chiswell Green, nr. St. Albans, Herts
3-4 Jun	**Pensthorpe Plant & Gardener's Fair** Pensthorpe Waterfowl Park, Fakenham, Norfolk
3-7 Jun	**Walpole St. Peter Annual Flower Festival** Church of St. Peter, Walpole St. Peter, Norfolk
4 Jun	**NCCPG Thymus Open Day** LW Plants, 23 Wroxham Way, Harpenden, Herts
9-11 Jun*	**Woburn Abbey Flower & Garden Show** Woburn, Beds
10 Jun	**Hoddesdon Festival of Gardening** Hoddesdon, Herts
11 Jun	**Aldham Village Gardens Open** Aldham, Essex
11 Jun	**Sisyrinchium Open Day** Jenny Burgess Alpines, 1 Rectory Cottage, Sisland, Norfolk
12 Jun-24 Jul	**Sculpture Exhibition** Feeringbury Manor, Coggeshall Road, Feering, Essex
16-18 Jun	**East of England Show** East of England Showground, Alwalton, nr. Peterborough, Cambs
16-18 Jun	**Essex County Show** Essex County Showground, Great Leighs, Essex
Mid Jun	**Iris Week** Alby Crafts & Gardens, Erpingham, Norfolk
18 Jun	**The Hidden Gardens of Bury St Edmunds** various venues, Bury St Edmunds, Suffolk
18 Jun	**Lavenham Village Gardens Open** Lavenham, Suffolk
18 Jun	**Nowton Country Fair** Nowton Road, Bury St Edmunds, Suffolk
21-22 Jun	**Lincolnshire Show** Lincolnshire Showground, Grange-de-Lings, Lincoln, Lincs

23-25 Jun	**The Anglian Flower & Garden Show** Bourn Airfield, Bourn, Cambs
23 Jun	**A Midsummer Wander through the Garden** Royal Horticultural Society's Garden 'Hyde Hall', Rettendon, Essex
24-25 Jun	**20 Eye Gardens Open** (*in aid of Eye Church*) Eye, Suffolk
24-25 Jun	**Festival of Gardening** Hatfield House, Hatfield Park, Hatfield, Herts
24-25 Jun	**Floral Festival** Benington Lordship Gardens, Benington, nr. Stevenage, Herts
24-25 Jun	**Ipswich Flower Show** Suffolk Showground, Bucklesham Road, Ipswich, Suffolk
24-25 Jun	**Rose & Sweet Pea Festival** Giffords Hall Vineyard & Sweet Pea Centre, Hartest, Suffolk
24 Jun	**Waltham Cross Festival of Gardening** Waltham Cross, Herts
25 Jun	**Chelsworth Village Gardens Open** Chelsworth, Suffolk
25 Jun	**Garden Open** The Priory, Stoke-by-Nayland, Suffolk
28 Jun-29 Jun	**Royal Norfolk Show** The Showground, Dereham Road, New Costessey, Norwich, Norfolk
28 Jun-1 Jul	**Wisbech Rose Fair** St. Peter's Parish Church, Church Terrace, Wisbech, Cambs

1-2 Jul	**Barrington Open Gardens** various venues, Barrington, Cambs
1-14 Jul	**Lavender Fair** part of Hitchin Festival, Herts
2 Jul*	**Chippenham Park Open Gardens** Chippenham, nr. Newmarket, Cambs
2 Jul	**Churches Together Millennium Celebration** Gardens of the Rose, Chiswell Green, nr. St Albans, Herts
2 Jul	**Ringstead Garden Sunday** various venues, Ringstead, Norfolk

14-16 Jul	**Hacheston Rose Festival** All Saints Church and surrounding fields, Hacheston, Suffolk
23 Jul	**Cowlinge Open Gardens Day** Cowlinge, nr Newmarket, Suffolk
26 Jul	**Sandringham Flower Show** Sandringham Park, Sandringham, Norfolk
29-30 Jul	**Capel Manor Fuchsia Show** Capel Manor Gardens, Bullsmoor Lane, Enfield, Middlesex
29 Jul-30 Jul	**The National Show for Miniature Roses** The Gardens of the Rose, Chiswell Green, nr. St. Albans, Herts

Beth Chatto Gardens, Essex

4 Aug-10 Sept (Fri, Sat, Sun)	**Lantern Lit Evening Garden** Pureland Japanese Garden, North Clifton, Lincs
5-6 Aug	**Thompson and Morgan Open Weekend** Poplar Lane, Ipswich, Suffolk
19-20 Aug	**British Gladiolus Society Show** Capel Manor Gardens, Bullsmoor Lane, Enfield, Middlesex
22-23 Aug	**English Wine Festival** New Hall Vineyard, Chelmsford Road, Purleigh, Essex
26-28 Aug	**Autumn Garden Festival** Audley End House & Gardens, Essex
26-27 Aug	**Ely Horticultural Show** Ely, Cambs
27-28 Aug	**The Countess of Warwick Country Fair** Little Easton Manor Gardens, Little Easton, nr. Dunmow, Essex
27-28 Aug	**Walsham le Willows Village Gardens Open** Walsham le Willows, Suffolk

2-3 Sept	**Boston Horticultural Show** Central Park, Boston, Lincs
3 Sept	**Hall Farm Garden Open Day** *(for National Gardens Scheme)*, Harpswell, Gainsborough, Lincs
3 Sept	**Plant Fair** Elgood's Brewery Gardens, North Brink, Cambs
4-5 Sept	**Autumn Garden Weekend** Bressingham Gardens & Steam Museum, Bressingham, nr. Diss, Norfolk
6 Sept	**Belton Garden Tour** Belton House, Park & Gardens, Belton, nr. Grantham, Lincs
16-17 Sept	**Cambridgeshire Autumn Garden & Interiors Show** Huntingdon Racecourse, Cambs
16 Sept	**Royal Horticultural Society's Garden 'Hyde Hall'** NCCPG Plant Sale, Rettendon, Essex
17 Sept	**Monksilver Nursery Open Day** Oakington Road, Cottenham, nr. Cambridge, Cambs
17 Sept	**Plant Sale** Ickworth House, Park & Gardens, Horringer, Suffolk
30 Sept-1 Oct	**Norfolk Autumn Garden & Interiors Show** Fakenham Racecourse, Norfolk

15 Oct*	**Chippenham Park Open Gardens** Chippenham, nr. Newmarket, Cambs
22 Oct-30 Nov	**Autumn Colours** Fairhaven Woodlands and Water Gardens, School Road, South Walsham, Norfolk
22 Oct	**Autumn Colours** Kings Arms Path Garden, Kings Arms Yard, Ampthill
29 Oct	**The Beale Arboretum Open Day** West Lodge Park, Hadley Wood, nr. Barnet, Herts
29 Oct	**Mannington Gardens Open Day** *(for National Gardens Scheme)*, Mannington Hall, Norwich, Norfolk

CALENDAR
of the
Seasons

Discover the 'seasons of the garden', with this special calendar indicating the key highlights of the year – from the best time to see a certain plant, to a selection of places in the East of England where you can view that particular plant, flower or shrub at its best.

To help you find out more information about the gardens, they are colour coded according to the section they appear in within this guide. A key to the colour codes is shown below:

Lincolnshire and Cambridgeshire
Norfolk and Suffolk
Bedfordshire, Essex and Hertfordshire

Spring (*Mar-May*)

Highlights:- Bulbs come alive into colourful Daffodils, Tulips, Crocuses and Hyacinths. Early bedding plants in bloom, such as Wallflowers. Herbaceous borders starting to flower. Rockies are alive with miniature alpine flowers. Trees in blossom (Cherries, Crab Apples and Horse Chestnuts). Woodlands are carpeted with Bluebells and Fritillaries

FLOWER/PLANT/ SHRUB TO VIEW	BEST TIME TO VIEW	WHERE THE FLOWER/PLANT/SHRUB CAN BE VIEWED
Azalea	May-Jun	Blakenham Woodland Garden, Blickling Hall, Park and Garden, Fritton Lake, Hoveton Hall Gardens, Raveningham Hall Gardens Sheringham Park, The Beale Arboretum, Beth Chatto Gardens, Colchester Castle Park, Hylands Park
Bluebell	Apr-May	Elton Hall, Stable Studios, Blakenham Woodland Garden, Blickling Hall, Park and Garden, Boyton Vineyard, Haughley Park, Natural Surroundings, Ashridge Estate, Belfairs Park & Nature Reserve, Hatfield Forest National Nature Reserve, Hedingham Castle, RSPB The Lodge Reserve
Camellia	Apr-May	The Manor, The Villa, Blakenham Woodland Garden, Blickling Hall, Park and Garden, East Bergholt Place Garden, Felbrigg Hall, Gardens and Park, Hatfield House Garden, Layer Marney Towers, Oaklands Park
Clematis	Apr-Oct	The Crossing House, Docwra's Manor Gardens, Weavers Cottage, Houghton House, Little Hall, Sun House, Thorncroft Clematis Nursery, BBC Essex Garden, Feeringbury Manor, Hatfield House Garden
Cowslip	Apr-May	Anglesey Abbey and Gardens, The Butterfly & Wildlife Park, Candlesby Herbs, Prebendal Manor 14thC Gardens, Wimpole Hall, Park and Gardens, Gifford's Hall Vineyard & Sweet Pea Centre, Natural Surroundings, Oxburgh Hall, Gardens and Estate, Pensthorpe Waterfowl Park, Hatfield Forest National Nature Reserve, Hitchin Museum Physic Garden

Daffodil	Mar-Apr	Anglesey Abbey & Gardens, Auborn Hall Gardens, Elsham Hall Country & Wildlife Park, Grimsthorpe Castle, Gunby Hall, Springfields, Wimpole Hall, Park and Gardens, Blickling Hall, Park and Garden, Bradenham Hall Garden & Aboretum, Elsing Hall, Gainsborough's House, Ickworth House, Park and Gardens, Kentwell Hall, Nowton Park, Oxburgh Hall, Gardens and Estate, Walsingham Abbey Grounds, Wyken Hall, Elms Farm, Felsted Vineyards, Knebworth House Gardens & Park, Little Easton Manor Gardens, Woburn Abbey
Iris	May-Jul	Doddington Hall & Gardens (Flag), Elgoods Brewery Garden, The Manor, 'Pureland' Japanese Garden, Alby Crafts and Gardens, Helmingham Hall Gardens, Landmark Gardens, Melford Hall, Layer Marney Tower, Glen Chantry, Maldon Millennium Garden, Myddelton House Gardens (Bearded)
Magnolia	May-Jun	Elton Hall, Blakenham Woodland Garden, East Bergholt Place Garden, Priory Park, St Pauls Walden Bury, Tymperleys
Primula	Mar-May	The Manor, Fairhaven Woodland & Water Gardens (Candelabra), Little Hall, Woottens Plants, Benington Lordship Gardens, LW Plants
Rhododendron	Apr-Jun	Blickling Hall, Park and Garden, East Bergholt Place Garden, Fairhaven Woodland & Water Gardens, Fritton Lake, Haughley Park, Hoveton Hall Gardens, Mannington Gardens, Sandringham, Sheringham Park, Somerleyton Hall & Gardens, Ashridge, The Beale Arboretum, Belfairs Park & Nature Reserve, Cheslyn Gardens, Kings Arms Path Garden, The Swiss Garden
Tulip	Apr-mid May	Anglesey Abbey and Gardens, Ascoughfee Hall, Docwra's Manor Garden, Springfields, The Abbey Gardens, Hales Hall Garden & Historic Barn, The Rookery Garden & Vineyard, Sun House, Gadebridge Park, Gardens of Easton Lodge, Park Farm, Saling Hall
Wisteria	May-Jun	Anglesey Abbey and Gardens, Peckover House, 'Pureland' Japanese Garden, East Ruston Old Vicarage Garden, Harling Vineyards, Holkham Nursery Gardens, Oxburgh Hall, Gardens and Estate, Somerleyton Hall & Gardens, Thrigby Hall Wildlife Gardens Hedingham Castle, Hylands Park, Mark Hall Gardens, Paycockes, Stockwood Craft Museum & Gardens, Wickham Place Farm

17

cont.

Early Summer (*Jun*)

Highlights:- Fields alive with the bright red of Poppies. Lovely Sweet Peas in the garden. Many fine Roses coming into bloom (mid June onwards). Numerous shrubs in flower (Summer Jasmine and Honeysuckle). Perennials creating spectacular displays in herbaceous borders

Dahlia	Jun-Oct	Anglesey Abbey and Gardens, Belton House, Blickling Hall, Park and Garden, East Ruston Old Vicarage Garden, Euston Hall, Felbrigg Hall, Gardens and Park, Oxburgh Hall, Gardens and Estate, Colchester Castle Park
Foxglove	Jun-Jul	Docwra's Manor Garden, Elton Hall, Bressingham Gardens and Steam Museum, Fairhaven Woodland & Water Garden, The Heraldic Garden & Lady Hilda Memorial Aboretum, "Magpies" Garden & Unusual Hardy Plant, Mickfield Watergarden Centre Nursery, Pilgrims' Herb Garden, Gardens of the Rose, Marks Hall Estate & Arboretum, RSPB The Lodge Reserve
Fuchsia	Jun-Oct	Kathleen Muncaster Fuchsias, Wimpole Hall, Park & Gardens, Blickling Hall, Park & Garden, Boyton Vineyard, Oxburgh Hall, Gardens & Estate, Sandringham, Thrigby Hall Wildlife Gardens, Beth Chatto Gardens, Clifftop Gardens
Geranium	Jun-Oct	Anglesey Abbey and Gardens, Ayscoughfee Hall, Docwra's Manor Garden (Meadow Cranesbill), Monksilver Nursery, The Stables Studio, Blickling Hall, Park and Garden, Bressingham Gardens and Steam Museum (Hardy), Elmhurst Park, Houghton Hall, Ickworth House, Park and Gardens, King's House Garden, Landmark Gardens, Magpie's Garden & Unusual Hardy Plant Nursery, Priory Maze & Gardens, Woottens Plants (Pelargoniums), Bedford Embankment Gardens, Clacton Seafront Gardens, Kings Arms Path Garden, Little Easton Manor Gardens, Prittlewell Square, Southchurch Park, Tower Gardens
Honeysuckle	Jun-Sept	Butterfly & Wildlife Park, Weavers Cottage Bruisyard Vineyard & Herb Garden, Hales Hall Garden & Historic Barn, Raveningham Hall Gardens, Somerleyton Hall & Gardens, BBC Essex Garden, Feeringbury Manor, Felsted Vineyards, Paycockes
Poppy	Jun	The Crossing House, Blickling Hall, Park and Garden, Brandon Country Park, Fritton Lake, The Heraldic Garden & Lady Hilda Memorial Arboretum, Natural Surroundings, Wingfield Old College & Gardens, Central Park (Chelmsford), Felsted Vineyards, Forge Museum & Victorian Cottage Garden, Wardown Park

18

cont.

| Rose | Jun-Jul | (see 'The Rose Trail' starting on page 21) |

Sweetpea   Jun-Sept   Wimpole Hall, Park and Gardens, Gifford's Hall Vineyard & Sweet Pea Centre, Oxburgh Hall, Gardens and Estate, Felsted Vineyards, Hatfield House Garden

Late Summer to Autumn (Jul-Sept)

Highlights:- Best displays of Begonias, Busy Lizzies, Fuchsias and Geraniums. Colourful Chrysanthemums brighten up the garden. Sweet-smelling Lavender is ready for harvest. Giant Sunflowers and Water Lilies bloom. Herb gardens are alive with bees and butterflies. Fields and orchards are laden with fresh vegetables and fruit (Aug/Sept). Vineyards are preparing for their annual harvest of grapes. First sights of Autumn colours (Sept).

Butterfly Bush   Jul-Aug   The Butterfly and Wildlife Park, Elton Hall, Wimpole Hall, Park and Gardens, Alby Crafts & Gardens, Boyton Vineyard, The Heraldic Garden & Lady Hilda Memorial Aboretum, Sandringham, The Beale Arboretum, Bedford Butterfly Park, Belfairs Park & Nature Reserve, Priory Park, Woburn Abbey

Lavender   Jul-Aug   Candlesby Herbs, Herb Garden, Blickling Hall, Park and Garden, Boyton Vineyard, Brandon Country Park, Castle Acre Priory, Elmhurst Park, The Heraldic Garden & Lady Hilda Memorial Arboretum, Holkham Nursery Gardens, Home & Garden at Winter Flora, Jenny Burgess Alpines, Kentwell Hall, Landmark Gardens, Norfolk Lavender, Oxburgh Hall, Gardens and Estate, Pilgrim's Herb Garden, Wyken Hall, Abbey Gardens (Waltham), Clifftop Gardens, Knebworth House, Gardens & Park, Little Easton Manor Gardens, Mark Hall Gardens, Paycockes, RSPB The Lodge Reserve, Shaw's Corner, Stockwood Craft Museum & Gardens

Phlox   Jul-Aug   Doddington Hall & Gardens, Bradenham Hall Gardens & Arboretum, Fritton Lake, Houghton Hall, Sun House, Hatfield House Garden, Layer Marney Tower

Water Lily   Jul-Aug   Byways Water Gardens, 'Pureland' Japanese Garden, Blickling Hall, Park and Garden, Bruisyard Vineyard & Herb Garden, The Heraldic Garden & Lady Hilda Memorial Arboretum, Hoveton Hall Gardens, Mannington Gardens, Mickfield Watergarden Centre, Oxburgh Hall, Gardens and Estate, Benington Lordship Gardens, Churchill Gardens, The Gardens of Easton Lodge, Prittlewell Square

Winter (Oct-Feb)

Highlights:- Aconites, Anemones and Winter Pansies give the garden some colour. Holly and Mistletoe ready for Christmas. Spectacular displays of Snowdrops. Sweet-smelling Viburnums.Trees and shrubs decorated with frost.

Anemone	Feb-Apr	The Villa, Wimpole Hall, Park and Gardens, Alby Crafts & Gardens, Bressingham Gardens and Steam Museum, Ashridge Estate, Hatfield Forest National Nature Reserve
Holly	Oct-Dec	Central Park (Peterborough), Harling Vineyards, Natural Surroundings, Sun House, Cheslyn Gardens, Clifftop Gardens, Marks Hall Estate & Arboretum, Prittlewell Square, Southchurch Hall Gardens
Snowdrop	Jan-Mar	Anglesey Abbey and Gardens, The Crossing House, Elsham Hall Country & Wildlife Park, The Manor, Monksilver Nursery, Wimpole Hall, Park and Gardens, Blickling Hall, Park and Garden, Gainsborough's House, Oxburgh Hall, Gardens and Estate, Pensthorpe Waterfowl Park, Walsingham Abbey Grounds, Belfairs Park & Nature Reserve, Benington Lordship Gardens, The Gardens of Easton Lodge, Glen Chantry, Hedingham Castle, Myddelton House Gardens, Swiss Garden
Viburnum	Nov-Apr	Anglesey Abbey and Gardens, Blickling Hall, Park and Garden, Oxburgh Hall, Gardens and Estate, Chalkwell Park, Churchill Gardens, Hatfield House Garden, Tymperleys
Winter Aconites	Feb-Mar	Anglesey Abbey and Gardens, Weavers Cottage, Wimpole Hall, Park and Gardens, Abbey Gardens, Alby Crafts and Gardens, Blickling Hall, Park and Garden, Ickworth House, Park and Gardens, Oxburgh Hall, Garden and Estate, Walsingham Abbey Grounds, Benington Lordship Gardens, Betho Chatto Gardens, Feeringbury Manor, RSPB The Lodge Reserve
Winter flowering Jasmine	Nov-Mar	Anglesey Abbey and Gardens, Houghton Hall, Jenny Burgess Alpines, Oxburgh Hall, Gardens and Estate, Mark Hall Gardens, Oaklands Park, Priory Park
Winter Pansies	Jan-Mar	Asycoughfee Hall, Wimpole Hall, Park and Gardens, Blickling Hall, Park and Garden, Elmhurst Park, Sun House, Colchester Castle Park, Southchurch Park, Wardown Park

Please note - this is only a selection of the region's plants and the gardens they can be found in. Contact the many gardens listed in this guide for further information.

20

The Rose Trail

The sweet-smelling 'Queen of Flowers' – the Rose, has cultivated its English home in the East of England, and over the next three pages you can follow our special trail which takes you from the home of The Royal National Rose Society (and Britain's most spectacular collection of Roses) to smaller more intimate gardens full of charm and character. Discover famous Rose growers, get lost in a Tudor Rose maze or take a walk amongst the Roses in sweet-smelling fields. For more information about the gardens mentioned on these pages, please refer to their main entry within this guide.

The Royal National Rose Society – Chiswell Green, St. Albans, Hertfordshire AL2 3NR Tel: 01727 850461
The society was founded in 1876, by a group of rose growers and breeders. By the time of the First World War, 4,500 people had joined. In 1929 the first trial grounds were established, and in 1948 these were moved to Hertfordshire. However it was not until 1959, that the Society moved to its present site at Chiswell Green. Today the country's oldest and largest specialist horticultural society has the Queen Mother as its patron, and by the gracious command of H.M. The Queen, the Society became The Royal National Rose Society in 1965. The Society exists to promote the interest and love of the Rose everywhere and to serve its members.

Some of the gardens featured within this trail, have limited or restricted opening hours. We have indicated these with an *, and suggest you refer to their entry within this guide, to check opening times, before starting your journey.

STARTING POINT:
The Gardens of the Rose (Chiswell Green, nr. St. Albans, Hertfordshire)
Duration of trail: Five days
Mileage: 226 miles
Route of trail: The Gardens of the Rose – Knebworth House, Gardens and Park (Stevenage) – Mark Hall Gardens (Harlow) – The Royal Horticultural Society's Garden Hyde Hall (Rettendon) – *Elms Farm (Blackmore End) – Bridge End Gardens (Saffron Walden) – Kentwell Hall (Long Melford) – John Appleby Rose Garden (Bury St. Edmunds) – *Helmingham Hall Gardens (Helmingham) – Peter Beales Classic Rose Gardens (Attleborough) – Thorncroft Clematis Nursery (Reymerston) – *Elsing Hall (Elsing) – Mannington Gardens (Saxthorpe)

Day 1 – Chiswell Green (nr. St. Albans) to Harlow (36 miles)
Morning – start the day at **The Gardens of the Rose,** home to Britain's best collection of roses. Enjoy some morning coffee, then head into the city of St. Albans for lunch. Afternoon – leave St. Albans on the A1057 to Hatfield, and the junction with the A1(M). Take this north to junction 7, and the entrance to **Knebworth House, Gardens and Park,** where you can enjoy a stroll through the rose gardens, and have some afternoon tea. On leaving the park, return to the roundabout over the A1(M), going straight across onto the A602 towards the town of Ware. After ten miles, you reach the junction with the A10, follow this south for three miles, then take the A414 to the town of Harlow. Overnight – Harlow

Knebworth House Gardens & Park, Hertfordshire

R.H.S. Garden, Hyde Hall, Essex

Day 2 – Harlow to Saffron Walden (62 miles) Morning – take a stroll through the roses at **Mark Hall Gardens,** and enjoy some morning coffee in the town. Then follow the A414 across to Chelmsford, where you take the A130 south to the village of Rettendon. Visit the outstanding rose collection at **The Royal Horticultural Society's Garden Hyde Hall,** including lunch. Afternoon – when you are ready to leave Hyde Hall, retrace your steps back to Chelmsford and take the A131 north to Braintree. Pass through the town, leaving on the B1053 towards Finchingfield. After five miles, turn right along an unclassified road to the village of Blackmore End. Visit *Elms Farm with its National Collection of Rosa Bourboniana. Retrace your steps to the B1053, and follow this via Finchingfield (stopping for some afternoon tea) to Saffron Walden. Overnight – Saffron Walden

Day 3 – Saffron Walden to Bury St. Edmunds (36 miles) Morning – visit **Bridge End Gardens** with its collection of roses, and enjoy some morning coffee in the town. Leave Saffron Walden on the B1053 to Radwinter, here you bear left to join the B1054 to the junction with the A1307 (passing through Steeple Bumpstead). At the junction, turn right, then one mile later left, onto the A1092 to Long Melford, where you can have lunch. Afternoon – get lost in the Tudor rose maze at **Kentwell Hall,** followed by some afternoon tea. Then after your visit, follow the A134 north to the town of Bury St. Edmunds. Overnight – Bury St. Edmunds area

Day 4 – Bury St. Edmunds to Diss (40 miles) Morning – take a stroll through the **John Appleby Rose Garden** in Bury St. Edmunds, then enjoy some morning coffee and lunch in the town. Afternoon – leave Bury St. Edmunds on the A14 towards Ipswich. After approximately 15 miles (just after passing the town of Stowmarket), leave the A14 to join the A1120 towards Yoxford. The road crosses the A140, then about five miles later, turn right onto the B1077 to visit **Helmingham Hall Gardens** with its collection of old-fashioned roses. You can also have afternoon tea here. After your visit, head north along the B1077 to the town of Diss. Overnight – Diss area

Day 5 – Diss to Saxthorpe (52 miles) Morning – leave Diss on the B1077 north to Attleborough, to visit **Peter Beales Classic Rose Gardens** with their world famous collection. Enjoy some morning coffee, then follow the A11 towards Norwich. After six miles, turn left onto the B1135 towards East Dereham. Five miles later you reach the village of Reymerston, where you can pay a short visit to the sunken rose garden at **Thorncroft Clematis Nursery**. After your visit, continue along the B1135 to the town of East Dereham, for lunch. Afternoon – leave East Dereham on the B1147 to Swanton Morley. Here you turn right (along an unclassified road) to visit the lovely *Elsing Hall with its many old-fashioned roses. Then retrace your journey back to Swanton Morley and turn right onto the B1147 to Bawdeswell. At the junction with the B1067, turn right, then immediately left onto the B1145 towards Aylsham. After seven miles, turn left again onto the B1149 to Saxthorpe. End the day at **Mannington Gardens,** with their heritage rose displays. Enjoy some afternoon tea here.

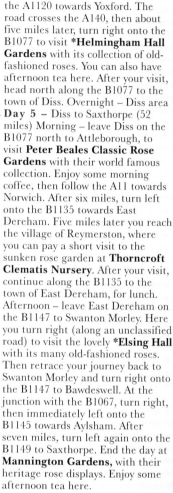

Mannington Gardens, Norfolk

22

During the Summer, why not pay a visit to a Rose field. Many members of the British Rose Growers Association open their fields to the public, either everyday or on special occasions. **Please note,** that although growers open their fields in June, the actual time of month this will commence, depends very much on weather conditions and location, but it is normally during the latter part. You are strongly advised to contact the numbers listed below to confirm details.

David Barnes (Holbeach, Lincs) – 01406 422459, Baytree Nurseries & Garden Centre (Weston, Lincs) – 01406 370242, Cants of Colchester (Colchester, Essex) – 01206 844008, Cley Nurseries Ltd (Cley-next-the-Sea, Norfolk) – 01263 740892, Godly's Roses (Redbourn, Herts) – 01582 792255, C. Gregory Roses (Weston, Lincs) – 01406 371633, Bill LeGrice Roses (Roughton, Norfolk) – 01263 833111, L W Van Geest (Farms) Ltd (Wykeham, Lincs) – 01775 725041, Warley Rose Gardens Limited (Great Warley, Essex) – 01277 221966.

BLICKLING HALL

Blickling Hall, Norfolk

The gardens surrounding Blickling Hall, a fine Jacobean mansion, include parterre and herbaceous borders, a secret garden with summer house and dry moat with scented plants, an 18th century temple and an orangery. Blickling is famous for its mature yew hedging and topiary. The garden has interest throughout the year.

Thanks to the foresight of the 11th Marquis of Lothian, and the inspiration of Mrs Norah Lindsay, well known in amateur landscaping at the time, the lay-out of the formal parterre garden at Blickling Hall was drastically altered in the early 1930's. The fussy and complicated network of numerous small beds and topiary, laid out for Constance, Lady Lothian in 1872, was considerably reduced and simplified, leaving four large square beds, flanked by rectangular beds of roses and catmint. On each corner and actually positioned in the rose beds, a yew bush stands in military fashion, acorn shaped and about twelve feet in height.

23

BLICKLING HALL

The small beds have been removed, the cleared areas were then levelled and turfed over, but even after some fifty years, the depressions are still clearly visible, and it is not difficult to pick out where many of the old flower beds used to be. The dense yew blocks shaped like grand pianos were also retained, and these stand aloof on their own areas of grass beyond the four square beds. Positioned in the centre of the main lawn is an attractive stone fountain, placed in its present position in 1872. The surrounding pool contains water lilies and goldfish, although unfortunately, the latter prove to be a tempting delicacy for the occasional passing heron. Circular in shape, the fountain succeeds nicely in breaking up the dominance of the many straight lines and angles contained in a formal garden.

The two beds nearest the House are a delightful blend of colours, predominately blue, mauve, pink and white. The two beds beyond are based on yellow and orange, and, rather surprisingly perhaps, there is no real clash of colour. The height grading of the herbaceous plants in the beds was extremely well thought out, giving the immediate impression that the soil in each bed is raised by two or three feet towards the centre. In actual fact, the difference in soil level is no more than about nine inches.

The considerable height in the middle of the beds is obtained by using such plants as Lavantera olbia 'Rosea'. Echinops ritro, (Globe Thistle), Campanula lactiflora and Delphinium. Sloping away from the centre and providing the intermediate height are Veronica in various forms, Lythrum saliceria 'Robert', Astrantia major, and Salvia. Towards the extreme outside are Geranium engressii, Stachys macrantha and Anaphalis margaritacea. These are only a few of the plants used in the lay-out, but the overall picture is most attractive, with the subtle blending of colours and prolonged period of flowering.

Bordering the first two beds are pink and crimson floribunda roses, 'Else' and 'Kirsten' Poulsen. These are old varieties dating back to the mid 1920's, but they still perform satisfactorily and their colours tone extremely well with the display of neighbouring massed flowers. Catmint (Nepeta Mussinii) provides a further blend of grey and mauve throughout the Summer, although this plant does tend to smother the lower growth of the roses in a good season. The beds furthest from the House are bordered with polyantha roses, 'Locarno' and 'Gloria mundi', red and orange respectively.

Maintenance of these four colourful beds and the impressive long border nearby follows a similar pattern each year and is a procedure which works well. All plants are cut down in November to within five or six inches of ground level and the beds are then raked clean. Because of the density of plant, there is no serious weed problem during the Summer, although these can soon appear nearer the outside of the beds when there is more light and space. Digging is always done in the Autumn, allowing the Winter frosts to break down the soil, leaving it in a nice friable condition by the Spring. Some plant dividing and reducing is also done at this stage, although it is safe policy to leave the more tender subjects until the following Spring, in case unexpected losses occur during the Winter months. Because of the proximity of the plants, digging in mushroom compost is a difficult operation, so it is simply spread on the surface and left to break down. Any dividing of the tender subjects is done in March or April, and losses replaced as necessary.

Staking the taller plants is carried out through May and June and at Blickling, pea-sticks are still used in preference to more modern methods. They are a most effective form of staking, unobtrusive to the eye and, fortunately, still readily obtainable. Another old practice still adopted here, is the use of white painted wooden labels. There is a certain amount of additional work involved with these, but they are more in keeping with all that is around them and many last for two full seasons. They are also helpful to the many thousands of visitors who view the gardens each year.

Alan Mason,
Garden Designer, Broadcaster and Gardening host

I had been gardening for 20 years and studying the subject for 8 years before I felt confident enough to design gardens for others and to call myself a garden designer. No matter how many books you read or lectures you hear, there is nothing better for improving gardening know-how than visiting good gardens and meeting real gardeners ... and then having a go, and making one or two mistakes along the way. The more you visit the more you learn. We are blessed with some fabulous gardens in this area and some of the friendliest and most helpful gardeners anywhere. So, next time you visit a garden, don't forget your notepad. You're sure to find a plant, an idea or simply an address of another garden worth visiting. It took me 30 years to discover that I enjoy visiting gardens so much I should make a career out of it. We now develop garden tours in this area as well as almost anywhere in Europe. Happy hunting.

ALAN'S FAVOURITE THREE PLANTS:
Hosta 'Frances Williams',
Physocarpus opulifolius 'Diabolo' and
Quercus suber (Cork Oak)

ALAN'S GARDENING HINT:
"When is the best time to take cuttings?"

"When someone offers them for free!"

Colour is the key to this area. The multi-coloured palette of the bulbfields in Spring. The vibrant yellow of Oilseed Rape, splashed across the Lincolnshire Wolds, in early Summer. Flower festivals galore. Huge auctions, markets and even wayside stalls, heaped with flowers and piled with succulent fruit and vegetables all grown in the rich dark brown peat of the Fens. This fertile land, which makes even green-fingered gardeners green-eyed with envy, was once just bog and marsh with a few islands inhabited by suspicious (some say web-footed!) people. Romans, Saxons, medieval monks all had a go at draining the land. But it took the famous Dutch engineers in the 17th century to finally succeed. Their influence lives on, not just in the architecture and the place names but in the glorious Daffodil and Tulip fields that cover vast areas of this grower's paradise. Discover the history in the Bulb Museum at Pinchbeck. While the flower parade at nearby Spalding is one of Britain's most colourful events with millions of Tulip heads decorating miles of spectacular floats.

You'll find more wonderful flower displays in the area's historic churches, including the peaceful charms of the churches in South Holland's Flower Festival.

Holland isn't the only country you'll be reminded of in this area. At 'The Lawn' in Lincoln, you'll find Sir Joseph Bank's Conservatory which houses exotic plants brought back from his voyage of discovery to the Antipodes with James Cook in 1768. The nearby John Dawber Garden features plants and settings which echo the city's links with towns in Germany, China and Australia, while the Japanese garden at Pureland offers a harmony of nature and inner peace with waterfalls, pagodas and a little tea bridge.

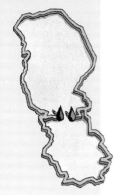

The Victorian walled kitchen garden at Normanby Hall, near Scunthorpe, is another fascinating renovation, filled with 19th century varieties of fruit, vegetables and flowers. Peckover House, in elegant Georgian Wisbech, boasts not just a walled garden but a fernery, orangery and croquet lawn, too.

Surrounded by fields of Roses, Wisbech is a treat, especially at Rose Fair time in early July. At Elgood's historic Brewery you can sample a glass of real ale and then admire the beautiful gardens with their fine specimen trees.

For green fingered students, why not start your gardening studies in Cambridge, amid the hushed charm of ancient College courtyard gardens or on the manicured lawns of "The Backs". Graduate to the wonderful Botanic Gardens with their National Collections and water, Winter and scented Gardens.

Water is the thing to drink at charming Woodhall Spa. The Victorians discovered its curative qualities and proceeded to build a fashionable spa town, complete with beautiful woodland walks where you can still stroll today. Turf mazes were an earlier fashion. The one at Hilton was built in the 17th century. The Yew Tree Avenue at Clipsham will take you back to stately days of horse and carriage. To the days of that most famous gardener of all, Capability Brown. Finish your tour with a pilgrimage to his tomb, at the church in the little village of Fenstanton.

On the following pages you will find information about many of the region's gardens, including contact details, directions, special features and facilities available. Shown below is a key to the symbols used on the entries. A map reference has been provided; to be used with the map on page 43. Prices shown are Adults/OAP's/Children. We do advise that you contact the individual gardens before visiting, to check opening times and admission prices as changes do occur after press date.

*Hall Farm,
Lincolnshire*

KEY TO SYMBOLS

- ❂ Member of the East of England Tourist Board
- 🎁 gift shop
- ❀ plants/produce for sale
- 🅿 parking
- 🚾 toilet facilities
- ☕ light refreshments/snacks
- ⛱ picnic area
- ✕ restaurant/tearoom
- 𝑘 pre-booked guided tours/talks
- 🐕 dogs permitted on lead
- ♿ disabled visitors welcome
- SE special events
- 🄶 connection to famous gardener

27

✤ **ARRINGTON** *(nr Royston)* *E12/13*
◉ WIMPOLE HALL, PARK AND
GARDEN (The National Trust),
ARRINGTON, NR. ROYSTON
CAMBRIDGESHIRE SG8 0BW
TEL: 01223 207257 FAX: 01223 207838
Eight miles southwest of Cambridge, off the A603
(junction 12 of the M11).

18th century house set in an extensive
wooded park, landscaped by Bridgeman,
Brown and Repton. Walks through gardens
and park. Daffodils in Spring, formal Dutch
gardens with Spring bulbs, Victorian
parterre and newly restored working vegetable
garden. **Features:** arboretum, garden
folly (in park), landscaped parkland, statuary/
sculpture and topiary. Dutch, kitchen,
parterre and Rose gardens. National
Collection of Walnuts (juglans).
🄶 - Lancelot 'Capability' Brown, Humphry
Repton and Charles Bridgeman. *Open: 18
Mar to 30 Jul, 2 Sept to 22 Oct daily except Mon
and Fri (open Good Fri and Bank Hol Mon). Aug
daily (not Mon) 1300-1700, 25 Oct to 5 Nov, Wed,
Sat and Sun 1300-1600. (Bank Hol Mon 1100-
1700). £5.90/ £5.90/£2.70* ♿ 🅿 ♿ ♨ 🍴 ✕ 🎁 ♿
SE - please telephone for details

✤ **CAMBRIDGE** *F12*
◉ CAMBRIDGE UNIVERSITY BOTANIC
GARDEN, CORY LODGE, BATEMAN
STREET, CAMBRIDGE CB2 1JF
TEL: 01223 336265 FAX: 01223 336278
Entrance in Bateman Street – 25 yards from A1309.

Forty acres of fine gardens with glasshouse,
including scented, dry, genetic, rock and
Winter gardens and lake, near the centre
of Cambridge. **Features:** Arboretum,
herbaceous borders, landscaped parkland,
maze (hedge) and tropical house. Rock/alpine,
Rose, scent, wildflower, water and woodland
gardens. National Collections of Fritillaria
(European species), Geranium (species and
primary hybrids), Lonicera (species and
primary hybrids), Ribes (species and primary
hybrids), Ruscus, Bergenia (species and

primary hybrids), Tulipa (species and
primary hybrids), Saxifraga (European species)
and Alchemilla. Special collections of
Lavender, Lime, Sorbus, English Natives
and Bearded Irises. *Open: All year, daily,
Summer 1000-1800; Winter 1000-1600. Closed
Christmas and Boxing Days. £2/£1.50/£1.50.*
♿ 🆆 ♿ 🍴 ✕ 🎁 ♿

✤ **COTON** *(nr. Cambridge)* *F12*
COTON ORCHARD,
MADINGLEY ROAD, COTON,
NR. CAMBRIDGE CB3 7PJ
TEL: 01954 210234 FAX: 01954 212332
Two minutes from junction 13 of M11, and A428.

Garden centre set in the middle of an
orchard. Licensed restaurant. Morning coffee.
Afternoon tea. Weekend roasts. Dried/silk
flowers, gifts and much more. *Open: Mon-
Sat 0900-1730, Sun 1030-1630. Late night
until 2000, Thurs and Fri. Admission free.* ♿ ♨
🅿 🆆 ♨ ✕ ♿

✤ **COTTENHAM** *(nr. Cambridge)* *F11*
MONKSILVER NURSERY,
OAKINGTON ROAD, COTTENHAM,
NR. CAMBRIDGE CB4 8TW
TEL: 01954 251555
*Leave A14 at first junction west of Cambridge,
between Oakington and Cottenham.*

Specialist nursery and garden. **Features:**
Herbaceous borders. National Collections
of Lamium (inc. Galeobdolon) and Vinca.
Special collections of Grasses, Ferns, Aster,
Sedum, Centaurea, Hemerocallis, Anthemis,
Campanula and Geranium. *Open: Mar-Jun
and Oct, Fri and Sat, 1000-1600. Admission free.*
♨ 🅿 🎄 SE - 17 Sept

Cambridge
One of Britain's most beautiful university
cities, with its historic colleges sitting
within a colourful patchwork of gardens,
public parks and ancient common land. "The
Backs" were developed in the 16th century
and are described as one of the world's
loveliest river settings. Here, you'll find wonderful
views of the colleges across immaculate lawns
and watermeadows, carpeted with flowers in
Spring. The colleges themselves are well-known
for their gardens. The ones at Christ's, Clare,
Emmanuel, Magdalene, Newnham Peterhouse,
Robinson, Selwyn and Sidney Sussex, are particularly
good. Although private, they will on occasions
open to the public. Elsewhere in the city,
don't miss the green open spaces of Christ's
Pieces, Coe Fen, Midsummer Common,
Jesus Green and Parker's Piece. While the
internationally renowned Botanic Garden is
second only in status to Kew.

✤ **ELSWORTH** *(nr. Cambridge)* *E11/12*
31 SMITH STREET, ELSWORTH,
NR. CAMBRIDGE CB3 8HY
TEL: 01954 267414 FAX: 01954 267414
From A428, turn left in Elsworth – second house on left.

Informal cottage garden of ³/₄ acre with herbaceous plantings, herbs and kitchen garden. **Features:** Herbaceous borders. Fruit and vegetable, herb, kitchen and scent gardens. National Collections of Artemisia and Nerum oleander. *Open: By appointment only, please telephone to confirm visit. £1/£1/free.*
✿ 🅿 �📶 🚹 ⅂ ₆

✤ **ELTON** *(nr. Peterborough)* *C/D9/10*
◉ ELTON HALL, ELTON,
NEAR PETERBOROUGH PE8 6SH
TEL: 01832 280468 FAX: 01832 280584
Near to A1, off A605 Peterborough to Oundle Road.

The romantic home of the Proby family for over 350 years, is a mixture of medieval, gothic and classical styles. Beautiful gardens. **Features:** Arboretum, garden folly, herbaceous borders, landscaped parkland, statuary/sculpture and topiary. Knot, parterre, Rose and sunken gardens. **G** - Humphry Repton. *Open: 28, 29 May; Wed in Jun; Wed, Thurs and Sun in Jul and Aug; Aug Bank Hol Mon, 1400-1700. Hall and gardens £5/£5/accompanied children free. Gardens only - £2.50/£2.50/children free (if accompanied by an adult)* ♿ ✿ 🅿 �📶 🚻 🏠 ✕ 🚹 *SE*

✤ **GODMANCHESTER** *(nr. Huntingdon)* *E11*
◉ ISLAND HALL, POST STREET,
GODMANCHESTER,
NR. HUNTINGDON PE18 8BA
TEL: 0171 491 3724 FAX: 0171 355 4006
In centre of Godmanchester, next to car park. One mile south of Huntingdon. Fifteen miles north west of Cambridge (A14).

A mid eighteenth century mansion of great charm owned and restored by an award winning interior designer and his family. Set in a tranquil riverside setting with formal gardens and ornamental island forming part of the grounds, in area of best landscape. *Open: Suns in Jul (2, 9, 16, 23 , 31) 1430-1700, last admittance is 1630. Groups, May to Sept (except Aug) by appointment. Grounds only £2/£2/£1.*
🅿 🚹

✤ **HEMINGFORD GREY** *(nr. Huntingdon)* *E11*
THE MANOR, HEMINGFORD GREY,
NR. HUNTINGDON PE19 9BN
TEL: 01480 463134 FAX: 01480 465026
Located north of the A14 – the turn-off for Hemingford Grey is marked.

The oldest continually inhabited house in England. Former home of Lucy Boston and setting for the Greene Knowe books. Magnificent collection of old Roses. **Features:** Herbaceous borders and topiary. Rose and scent gardens. Special collection of Irises. *Open: All year, garden 1000-1800. £1/£1/50p House strictly by appointment only.* ♿ ✿ 🚹 🐕 ⅂

HILTON *(nr. Huntingdon)* *E11*

HILTON TURF MAZE, THE GREEN,
HILTON, NR. HUNTINGDON
TEL: 01480 830137 – The Parish Clerk

In the village of Hilton, six miles south-east of Huntingdon on the B1040.

One of eight surviving turf mazes in England, cut in 1660 and scheduled as an Ancient Monument. In the centre stands a monument, commemorating the construction. **Features:** Maze (turf). *Open: Apr to Nov, daily, any reasonable time. Admission free.* P *(nearby)*

HUNTINGDON

QUEEN KATHERINE'S GARDEN,
BUCKDEN TOWERS,
BUCKDEN, HUNTINGDON,
PE18 9TA
TEL: 01480 810344 FAX: 01480 811918

Off A1, 2 miles south of A14 junction

Reconstruction of a Tudor period Knot garden in grounds of historic palace of Bishops of Lincoln. Now a Christian retreat and conference centre. **Features:** Knot garden and 15 acre park and garden. *Open: May to Sept, Wed-Sun 0900-1700. Minimum donation of 20p per person suggested.* P WC *(Sat, Sun, Bank Hol pm only)*

LINTON *G13*

CHILFORD HALL VINEYARD,
CHILFORD HALL,
BALSHAM ROAD, LINTON CB1 6LE
TEL: 01223 892641 FAX: 01223 894056

Follow brown tourist signs from A11 and A1307

Stroll around our vineyard trail, take a winery tour with tastings and a souvenir glass. Browse in the vineyard shop, and enjoy refreshments in the Vineleaf Cafe. **Features:** Statuary/sculpture and vineyard. *Open: Good Fri to 1 Nov, daily, 1100-1730. £4.50/£4.50/free.* P WC

LODE *(nr. Cambridge)* *F/G12*

ANGLESEY ABBEY AND GARDENS
(The National Trust), LODE,
NR. CAMBRIDGE CB5 9EJ
TEL: 01223 811200 FAX: 01223 811200

In village of Lode, six miles north-east of Cambridge on the B1102.

The house, dating from 1600 is surrounded by a magnificent ninety-eight acre landscaped garden and arboretum with statues. Hyacinths in Spring and magnificent herbaceous borders and Dahlia in Summer. One mile long Winter Walk. Working watermill in the grounds. **Features**: Arboretum,

herbaceous borders, landscaped parkland and statuary/sculpture. Winter garden. Special collection of Snowdrops. *Open: House 25 Mar to 22 Oct, Wed-Sun and Bank Hol Mon, 1300-1700. Winter garden 6 Jan to 24 Mar, Thur-Sun, 1030-dusk. All gardens 25 Mar to 2 Jul, Wed-Sun and Bank Hol Mon; 3 Jul to 17 Sept, daily, 20 Sept to 22 Oct, Wed-Sun, 1030-1730. Property closed on Good Friday. Last admission to property 1630, 25 Mar to 22 Oct. House and gardens, Adults/OAPs £6.10 (Wed-Sat), £7.10 (Sun, Bank Hol Mon). Children half price on all categories. Gardens only, Adults/OAPs £3.75, children half price. Winter garden, Adults/OAPs £3, children half price. Family tickets availabe.* P WC SE - throughout year, please telephone for details.

NASSINGTON *(nr. Peterborough)* *C9*

PREBENDAL MANOR 14TH CENTURY
GARDENS, CHURCH STREET,
NASSINGTON, NR. PETERBOROUGH
PE8 8QG TEL: 01780 782575

Eight miles west of Peterborough. Seven miles north of Oundle

Unique six acre recreated medieval garden, centred around a 13th century manor. Included in the visit is a 15th century dove-cote and tithe barn museum. **Features:** Vineyard. Fruit & vegetable, herb, kitchen, rose, wildflower and woodland gardens. *Open: Sun & Wed, May, June, Sept, 1400-1730, Sun, Wed & Thurs, July, Aug 1400-1730. £3/£3/£1.20* P WC

PETERBOROUGH *D9*

CENTRAL PARK, PARK CRESCENT,
PETERBOROUGH PE1 4DX
TEL: 01733 742543

Fifteen minutes walk from the city centre.

A Victorian park just fifteen minutes from the city centre. Tranquillity and activities for all the family, including a sunken garden. **Features:** Arboretum. Rose and sunken gardens. *Open: All year, daily, any reasonable time. Admission free.* WC

CAMBRIDGESHIRE

❖ **QUEEN ADELAIDE** (nr. Ely)   G10
THE HERB GARDEN,
DAIRY FARM HOUSE,
PRICKWILLOW ROAD,
QUEEN ADELAIDE, NR. ELY CB7 4SH
TEL: 01353 662559
One and a half miles east of Ely on the B1382.

Formal herb garden. Large wild garden and pond. **Features:** Herbaceous borders. Herb, water, wildflower and woodland gardens.
Open: by appointment only. Admission free. ✿ **P**

❖ **SHEPRETH** (nr. Cambridge)

THE CROSSING HOUSE,   F13
78 MELDRETH ROAD, SHEPRETH,
NR. CAMBRIDGE SG8 6PS
TEL: 01763 261071
Half a mile west of the A10, on Meldreth road level crossing.

Quarter of an acre cottage garden. Old fashioned plants and rarities, planted in abundance in box-edged beds. Pools, three greenhouses and alpine beds. **Features:** Herbaceous borders and topiary. Rock/alpine garden. *Open: All year, daily, dawn to dusk. Admission free (but collecting box for NGS).*
P *(on road)* 🚾 ⚲

LANCELOT 'CAPABILITY' BROWN (1716-1783)
One of Britain's most famous landscape designers, he got the nickname 'Capability' from his skill in suggesting how 'full capabilities' might be realised in his clients' gardens. Born in 1716, he rose from humble origins to be on familiar terms with the highest in the land. In the late 18th century, the fashion for fine formal gardens had given way to the Italian-inspired landscaped parkland and this type of gardening was Brown's speciality. His designs were usually based around three natural ingredients – water, trees and terrain, and throughout the region there are numerous places where you can see his work. In 1767, he used his modest fortune to acquire a property for his family in the village of Fenstanton, Cambridgeshire, where he became Lord of the Manor. He died on the 6th Feb. 1783, aged 67. You can pay your respects to this great gardener at his resting place at Fenstanton church.

DOCWRA'S MANOR GARDEN,   F13
2 MELDRETH ROAD, SHEPRETH,
NR. CAMBRIDGE SG8 6PS
TEL: 01763 260235
Half a mile west of the A10 (London to Cambridge Road). Four miles from junction with M11.

Set around an 18th century red-brick house are a series of walled gardens, containing many unusual and mixed herbaceous plants and shrubs. All year round interest. **Features:** Herbaceous borders. Walled garden. *Open: All year, Wed and Fri, 1000-1600. Also first Sun of month from Apr to Oct, 1400-1700. Or by appointment, (01763 261473/ 261557/260235). £2/£2/under 16 free. Additional charges for visit's out of hours and guided tours.* **P** 🚾 ⌂ ✗ ♿

❖ **SOHAM** (nr. Ely)   G11
BYWAYS WATER GARDENS,
BARCHAM ROAD, SOHAM,
NR. ELY CB7 5TU
TEL: 01353 721608 FAX: 01353 721609
Follow signs for Orchard Farm Business Park on the A142.

Water gardens, large Koi ponds and natural pond, with everything connected to water gardening. **Features:** Water garden. *Open: All year, daily, 0930-1730. Admission free.* ✿ **P** 🚾 ⚖ ♿

❖ **WEST WICKHAM** (nr. Cambridge) G12/13
WEAVER'S COTTAGE,
35 STREETLY END, WEST WICKHAM,
NR. CAMBRIDGE CB1 6RP
TEL: 01223 892399
Streetly End is halfway between Horseheath (on the A1307) and West Wickham.

Half acre garden exuberantly planted for fragrance, with Spring bulbs, shrubs, herbaceous plants, climbers, old roses, sunken and scree gardens. **Features:** Herbaceous borders. Rock/alpine, fruit and vegetable, scent and sunken gardens. National Collection of Lathyrus. *Open: Any reasonable time, by appointment only. £1/75p/50p.* 🚾 ✗ SE - 24 April

31

✤ **WEST WRATTING** *(nr. Cambridge)*   *G12*
PADLOCK CROFT,
PADLOCK ROAD, WEST WRATTING,
NR. CAMBRIDGE CB1 5LS
TEL: 01223 290383 FAX: 01223 290383
Plantsman's cottage garden, with hardy and half-hardy herbaceous and alpine plants. **Features:** Herbaceous borders. Kitchen, rock/alpine and woodland gardens. National Collections of Adenophora, Campanula, Platycodon and Symphyandra. Special collection of Bellflowers. *Open: All year, daily (except Sun) – by appointment only. £1/£1/£1.*
🌡 🅿 🎋 ⚔ ♿

✤ **WICKEN** *(nr. Ely)*   *G11*
◉ WICKEN FEN NATIONAL NATURE
RESERVE (The National Trust),
LODE LANE, WICKEN CB7 5XP
TEL: 01353 720274 FAX: 01353 720274
Three miles west of Soham in the village of Wicken on the A1123.

Britain's oldest Nature reserve and a haven for birds, plants, insects and mammals. Working windpump and restored Fen Cottage with garden, including rare plants e.g fen ragwort, violet and milk parsley; traditional droves and boardwalk. **Features:** Wildflower gardens. *Open: Fen Cottage – open Easter to Oct, Sun, 1400-1700. Reserve - daily, dawn-dusk, centre closed Mondays, Tue-Sun 1000-1700. Reserve and cottage – £3.70/£3.70/£1.20; cottage only £1.50/£1.50/£1.50.*
🏛 🅿 ♿ ♨ ⚔ 🐕 ♿ SE - please telephone for details

✤ **WILBURTON** *(nr. Ely)*   *F11*
HERB GARDEN,
NIGEL HOUSE, 67 HIGH STREET,
WILBURTON, NR. ELY CB6 3RA
TEL: 01353 740824
In the village of Wilburton – take A1123 from A10 roundabout. Situated near the church.

The garden is a herb garden, arranged in collections – culinary, astrological, medicinal, biblical, Shakespearian etc, with many old roses. **Features:** Herbaceous borders with aromatic plants, knot garden and old roses. *Open: May to Sept, most days (but please telephone first). Admission free.* 🌡 🅿 📟 ⚔ 🐕 ♿

Wisbech Roses

In the heart of a fruit and flower growing area, the prosperous town of Wisbech in Cambridgeshire is also the main Rose-growing area of the country, with hundreds of thousands of Rose bushes distributed nationwide each year, mainly by mail order. Each July, the town holds its annual Rose fair. This was started 35 years ago when rosebuds were sold in the church gardens to raise money for restoration work to the Church of St. Peter and St. Paul. Over the years, the festival has grown to become one of England's finest flower festivals with exotic blooms, flown in especially, and traditional British blooms brought together in themed displays.

✤ **WISBECH**   *F8/9*
◉ ELGOOD'S BREWERY GARDENS,
NORTH BRINK, WISBECH PE13 1LN
TEL: 01945 583160 FAX: 01945 587711
From the A47, follow signs to Wisbech. Garden is located on the North Brink of river.

Four acres incorporating lawns, lake, maze, formal and informal areas, in a peaceful setting behind the family brewery. Unusual,

mature trees include Gingko, Tulip, Ailanthus, Walnut, Cedar and Monkey Puzzle in spacious, quiet town garden. Access to shop and paths are suitable for wheelchairs. **Features:** Maze (hedge) and tropical house. Herb, Japanese, rock/alpine and Rose gardens. *Open: 29 Apr to 1 Oct, Wed-Sun and Bank Hol Mon, 1300-1700. £2/£1.50/£1.50.* ⚫ ✿ 🅿 ᵂᶜ ☕ 🏛 ✕ ♿ SE - plant fair 14 May, 3 Sept

⊛ **PECKOVER HOUSE AND GARDEN** *F8/9*
(The National Trust), NORTH BRINK,
WISBECH PE13 1JR
TEL: 01945 583463 FAX: 01945 583463
On the north bank of the River Nene in Wisbech (B1441).

An outstanding Victorian garden with Orangery, Summer houses, Roses, herbaceous borders, fernery, croquet lawn and Reed barn. Georgian town house. **Features:** Herbaceous borders, flat maze (set in granite), topiary and tropical house. Herb and Rose Gardens. Victorian fernery, Orange tree and orchard. Special collections of Roses (seventy varieties), Malmaison Carnations and Regal Pelargoniums. Recreation of Victorian Garden pond. *Open: House and Garden – 1 Apr to 31 Oct, Sat, Sun, Wed and Bank Hol Mon, 1230-1730. Garden only – 1 Apr to 31 Oct, Mon,Tues,Thur, 1230-1730. House & Garden £3.80/£3.80/£1.75 (£2.50 on Garden only days).* ⚫ ✿ 🅿 *(in town)* ᵂᶜ ☕ ✕ ⚘ ♿ *(to garden only) SE* - phone for details

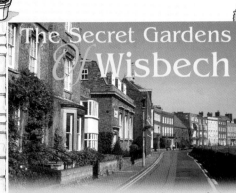

The Secret Gardens of Wisbech

Hidden behind the elegant facade of the Georgian North Brink are two secret gardens waiting to be discovered. The Victorian style walled garden at Peckover House (N.T.) has fruiting orange trees, unusual summer houses and colourful borders. Just a short stroll away the 200 year old North Brink Brewery (Elgoods Ales) has an attractive restored garden where old and new features blend delightfully together.

For Information Tel 01945 583263
Wisbech Tourist Information Centre
2-3 Bridge Street Wisbech PE13 1EW

AUBOURN *(nr. Lincoln)* *B/C5*

AUBOURN HALL GARDEN, HARMSTON ROAD, AUBOURN, NR. LINCOLN LN5 9DZ
TEL: 01522 788270

Seven miles south west of Lincoln, turn off A607 at Harmston, or A46 (through Haddington).

Beautiful red-brick Elizabethan manor house with three acres of garden, including herbaceous borders, lawns, shrubs, Rose and water gardens. **Features:** Herbaceous borders. Dell, rose and water gardens. *Open: Jul and Aug, every Wed, 1400-1730. £3/£2.50.*

BELTON *(nr. Grantham)* *B/C6/7*

BELTON HOUSE (The National Trust), BELTON, NR. GRANTHAM NG32 2LS
TEL: 01476 566116 FAX: 01476 579071

Three miles north of Grantham, on the A607 (Grantham to Lincoln road).

Thirty five acres containing formal and informal areas: Italian garden with fountain and restored, well-planted Orangery. Dutch garden with parterres and topiary. Statue walk. 'Eyecatcher' temple next to canal. Pleasure grounds with bulb and wildflower areas. Set within a beautiful parkland with lake, avenues and Bellmount Tower. **Features:** Garden folly, herbaceous borders, landscaped parkland, statuary/ sculpture and topiary. Dutch, Italian, and wildflower gardens. *Open: 1 Apr to 31 Oct, daily (except Mon/Tues). House, 1300-1730; Garden and Park, 1100-1730. Open Bank Hol Mon, but closed Good Fri. £5.30/£2.60.* SE - 26 Apr, 6 Sept

BRIGG *C2*

ELSHAM HALL COUNTRY AND WILDLIFE PARK, BRIGG DN20 0QZ
TEL: 01652 688698 FAX: 01652 688240

Off M180, Humber Bridge (junction 5). Follow brown signs.

Pretty lakeside gardens with Spring bulbs, May blossoms and Summer butterfly garden. Falconry centre, children's zoo, playground, craft and garden centre. Famous carp lake. **Features:** Arboretum and landscaped parkland. Butterfly, wild-flower and woodland gardens. Special collection of Narcissi (fifty varieties) and Elwes Snowdrop. G - Mark Chapman. *Open: Easter to mid Sept, daily, 1100-1700. £3.95/£3.75/ £2.50.* SE - throughout year, please telephone for details

CANDLESBY *(nr. Spilsby)* *F5*

CANDLESBY HERBS, CROSS KEYS COTTAGE, CANDLESBY, NR. SPILSBY PE23 5SF
TEL: 01754 890211 FAX: 01754 890211

One mile north from the Gunby roundabout, on the A1028.

Herb nursery with herbal workshop and craftwork. **Features:** Herbaceous borders. Herb and scent gardens. *Open: All year, daily, 1000-1700. Closed Mon, except Bank Hols. Admission free.*

CLIPSHAM *(nr. Stamford)* *C8*

CLIPSHAM YEW TREE AVENUE, CLIPSHAM, NR. STAMFORD
TEL: 01780 444394 –
Forestry Commission

Five miles north of Stamford, leave A1 at Stretton and follow road to Clipsham. The avenue is less than a mile from the village, on the road towards Little Bytham.

Unique avenue with 150 yew trees, over 200 years old, and stretching half a mile along the former carriage drive to Clipsham Hall. They are clipped annually into varied and bizarre shapes. **Features:** Topiary. *Open: All year, daily, any reasonable time. Admission free.*

✤ **DODDINGTON** *(nr. Lincoln)*   *B4/5*
DODDINGTON HALL AND GARDENS,
DODDINGTON, NR. LINCOLN LN6 4RU
TEL: 01522 694308 FAX: 01522 682584
*From A46 Lincoln by-pass, turn west onto B1190
for two miles.*

Doddington Hall is a superb Elizabethan
mansion which stands today as it was
completed in 1600. The walled gardens are
a delight at all times of year. **Features:**
Garden folly, herbaceous borders and maze
(turf). Statuary/sculpture collections and topiary.
Herb, knot, parterre (box), water and wildflower gardens. Special collection of semi-
naturalised Crown Imperial Lilies. *Open:
Gardens only – 20 Feb to 30 Apr, Sun, 1400-1800.
House and Gardens – May to Sept, Wed, Sun and
Bank Hol Mon, 1400-1800. Garden – £2.15/£2.15/
£1.10, House & Garden - £4.30/£4.30/£2.15.* ⚜ 🅿 ♿
♨ 🗚 ♿

✤ **GRIMSTHORPE** *(nr. Bourne)*   *C7/8*
☸ GRIMSTHORPE CASTLE,
GRIMSTHORPE, NR. BOURNE PE10 0NB
TEL: 01778 591205 FAX: 01778 591259
Situated on A151 midway between the A1 and Bourne.

Fifteen acres of formal and woodland
gardens including bulbs and wildflowers.
Fine topiary, Roses and herbaceous borders.
Unusual ornamental vegetable garden.
Features: Herbaceous borders, landscaped
parkland and topiary. Fruit and vegetable,
kitchen, Rose, wildflower and woodland
gardens. 🄶 - John Fowler. *Open: Easter Sun to
end Sept, Sun, Thurs and Bank Hols. Daily in
Aug (except Fri and Sat). 1300-1800. £3/£2/£1.50.*
⚜ 🅿 ♿ ♨ 🗚 ✕ 🏃 🐕 *(not in garden)* ♿

✤ **GUNBY** *(nr. Spilsby)*   *B8*
GUNBY HALL
(The National Trust)
GUNBY, NR. SPILSBY PE23 5SS
TEL: 01909 486411 – The National Trust
(regional office) FAX: 01909 486377
Seven miles west of Skegness on south side of A158

A fine red-brick house (dating from 1700),
and set in parkland. Many of the rooms are
panelled and there is a beautiful Oak stair-
case, as well as fine paintings, items of
furniture and china. The exquisite walled
garden is planted with traditional English
vegetables, fruit and flowers. **Features:**
Herbaceous borders. Fruit and vegetable,
herb, kitchen, Rose and wildflower gardens.

*Open: 5 Apr to end Sept. House – Wed, 1400-1800.
Garden – Wed and Thurs, 1400-1800. Also open
on Tues, Thurs and Fri, by written appointment
only with Mr J D Wrisdale at above address.
House and gardens -£3.60/£1.80. Gardens only
£2.60/£1.30.* ♨ 🅿 ♿ 🐕 *(in garden only)*

✤ **HARPSWELL** *(nr. Gainsborough)*   *B/C3*
HALL FARM GARDEN,
HARPSWELL,
NR. GAINSBOROUGH DN21 5UU
TEL: 01427 668412 FAX: 01427 667478
Seven miles east of Gainsborough on A631.

One and a quarter acre garden, including
pond, sunken, courtyard, Rose and walled
gravel gardens. Large range of old Roses,
shrubs and perennials – many unusual.
Features: Herbaceous borders. Rose and
sunken gardens. *Open: All year, daily, 1000-
1700. Please telephone to confirm opening times
in Winter. Admission free (but donations welcome
for NGS).* ♨ 🅿 ♿ 🗚 🐕 ♿ SE - 5 Sept

LINCOLNSHIRE

✲ **HEMSWELL** *(nr. Gainsborough)*   B/C3
MARTIN NEST NURSERIES,
HEMSWELL,
NR. GAINSBOROUGH DN21 5UP
TEL: 01427 668369 FAX: 01427 668369
www.martin-nest.demon.co.uk
Six miles east of Gainsborough on the A631.

Alpine nursery, with Primulas, Alpines and
Saxifages. **Features:** National Collection
of Primula auricula (show and alpine) –
come and see them in flower from mid Apr
to mid May. *Open: All year, daily, 1000-1630.*
Admission free. 🅿 ♿

✲ **LINCOLN**

◉ THE LAWN, UNION ROAD,   C4
LINCOLN LN1 3XY
TEL: 01522 560306/560330
*Follow brown 'Historic Lincoln' signs to uphill
area, and then to The Lawn.*

Formerly Lincoln's mental hospital, the
site includes landscaped gardens, The Sir
Joseph Banks Tropical Conservatory and
the John Dawber garden. **Features:**
Landscaped parkland, statuary/sculpture
and tropical house. Australian, fern,
German, old English, Phoenix, Russian
and water gardens. **G** - Sir Joseph Banks.
*Open: All year, Mon-Thurs, 0900-1700. Fri,
Summer 0900-1700, Winter 0900-1630. Sat and
Sun, Summer 1000-1700, Winter 1000-1600.*
Admission free. ♿ 🅿 ♿ ⚓ 🍴 ✕ ♿

◉ LINCOLN MEDIEVAL   C4
BISHOP'S PALACE (English Heritage),
MINSTER YARD,
LINCOLN LN2 1PU
TEL: 01522 527468
In city centre, on south side of Lincoln Cathedral.

Remains of a medieval palace of the
Bishops of Lincoln. Within its walls is one of
the most northerly vineyards in Europe.
Features: Vineyard. *Open: 1 Apr to 31 Oct,
daily, 1000-1800 (1700 in Oct). 1 Nov to 31 Mar,
Sat and Sun only, 1000-1600. Open daily for
Lincoln Christmas market. Closed 24-26 Dec &
1 Jan 2001 £1.90/£1.40/£1.* ♿ 🍴

✲ **LONG SUTTON** *(nr. Spalding)*   F8
◉ THE BUTTERFLY AND
WILDLIFE PARK, LONG SUTTON,
NR. SPALDING PE12 9LE
TEL: 01406 363833 FAX: 01406 363182
One mile off A17 at Long Sutton.

Set in twenty five acres, with herbaceous,
shrub and alpine gardens. Huge display of
Summer wildflowers. Hundreds of tropical
plants and shrubs in the butterfly house.
Features: Herbaceous borders, landscaped parkland and tropical house. Herb,
rock/alpine and wildflower gardens. Special
collection of Cowslips (the largest single
area in country). *Open: End Mar to end Oct,
daily from 1000. £4.80/£4.50/£3.20/£14 (family
ticket).* ♿ ❀ 🅿 ♿ ⚓ 🍴 ✕ 🐕 ♿

SPALDING - the centre of the British bulb industry
Since the end of the 19th century, Spalding has been at the centre of the British bulb
industry. Here, during the early Spring, the fields burst into vibrant colour as millions of Daffodil
and Tulip bulbs come into flower. The town is situated in the distinctive flat landscape of the
Fens. Once almost entirely flooded, it has been drained over the centuries with a system of
rivers and dykes, leaving a silt soil excellent for bulb growing. In 1890, commercial bulb
growing began and by the 1920's and 30's the fields were full of Tulips – and visitors, too, who
came to view the annual spectacle. But in the following years, more growers moved to the dry
bulb trade, as opposed to growing bulbs for flowers. To promote growth of the bulb, they
removed the tulip heads so the wonderful displays in the fields were reduced. And so were
the visitors – and subsequent business they brought with them. In 1959, a novel way was
suggested of not only using the millions of removed flower heads but also attracting back the
visitors. This was the birth of the famous Spalding Flower Festival. Every year since, floats
decorated with as many as half a million Tulip heads parade through the town, while in the
surrounding area, the local churches hold magnificent flower festivals. In 1964, a twenty-two
acre site was transformed into Springfield's, a showground planted with millions of bulbs and
dedicated to the promotion, study and practice of horticulture – especially the cultivation and
development of flowers grown from bulbs and corms.

✤ **MARTIN** *(nr. Lincoln)*   *D5*
THE STABLES STUDIO,
94 HIGH STREET, MARTIN,
NR. LINCOLN LN4 3QT
TEL: 01526 378528
On the B1191 between Metheringham and Woodhall Spa.

A small sculpture garden entitled 'Sculpture in the Wild'. A wild area is planted with native wild flowers and trees. Borders display a wide variety of plants. **Features:** Statuary/sculpture. Wildflower garden *Open: Apr to Sept, daily, 1000-1900. Admission free.* ♿ ♣ 🅿 🆆🅲 ✗ ☇ ♿

✤ **MORTON** *(nr. Gainsborough)*   *B3*
KATHLEEN MUNCASTER FUCHSIAS,
18 FIELD LANE, MORTON,
NR. GAINSBOROUGH DN21 3BY
TEL: 01427 612329
From A158 take 'C' road to Walkerith. Field Lane is on left.

Large collection of Hardy Fuchsias, permanently planted out in gardens, plus a Hardy Species section. Five hundred other stock plants displayed outside during summer. *Open: During the summer (until 15 Jul), daily (except Tues and Wed), 1000-dusk. After 15 Jul, please telephone first. Admission free.* ♣ 🅿 🆆🅲 🛆 *(pre-booked coach parties only)* ✗ ☇ ♿

✤ **NORMANBY** *(nr. Scunthorpe)*   *B1*
NORMANBY HALL COUNTRY PARK
(VICTORIAN KITCHEN GARDEN),
NORMANBY,
NR. SCUNTHORPE DN15 9HU
TEL: 01724 720588 FAX: 01724 721248
Four miles north of Scunthorpe on the B1430.

Fully restored and working walled kitchen garden, growing Victorian varieties of fruit, vegetables and flowers as if for "The Big House". **Features:** Fruit and vegetable and kitchen gardens. *Open: All year, daily, 1100-1700 (last admission 1630). Garden closes at 1600 in Winter (last admission 1530). £2.50/ £1.50/£1.50/under fives free (1998 prices). 50% discount for North Lincolnshire residents.* ♿ ♣ 🅿 🆆🅲 🛆 🗙 ✗ ☇ ♿

✤ **NORTH CLIFTON** *(nr. Newark)* *B4*
PURELAND 'JAPANESE GARDEN',
NORTH CLIFTON, NR. NEWARK
NG23 7AT TEL: 01777 228567
Signposted off the A1133, half way between Newark & Gainsborough

Harmony of nature and inner peace of man. Reflections of the landscape of Japan with hilocs, ponds, pagoda, bridges, waterfall, stepping stones and Koi carp. Cherry Trees, Bamboo, Aisa, Wisteria, Iris etc. Also Zen Garden and Japanese tea house. **Features:** Garden folly (pagoda), Maze (path) and statuary/sculpture (Budda's). 🅶 *Open: Apr 1-31 Oct, Tues-Fri, 1100-1730. Sat, Sun and Bank Hols, 1030-1730. Closed on Mon. £3.50/£2.50/ £1.50.* 🅿 🆆🅲 🛆 🗙 ✗ ☇ SE - Lantern lit evening garden, every weekend in Aug, and 1 & 2 weekend in Sept.

✤ **PINCHBECK** *(nr. Spalding)*

THE SPALDING BULB MUSEUM *E7*
& HORTICULTURAL EXHIBITION
(BIRCHGROVE GARDEN CENTRE),
SURFLEET ROAD, PINCHBECK,
NR. SPALDING PE11 3XY
TEL: 01775 680490 FAX: 01775 680656
On the old A16 between Pinchbeck and Surfleet.

Fascinating museum, depicting through photographs and artefacts, the history of the Lincolnshire bulb industry from 1880 to the present day. Adjoining garden centre. **Features:** Woodland and water garden. *Open: All year, daily, 0900-1700. Admission free.* ♿ ♣ 🅿 🆆🅲 🛆 🗙 ✗ ☇ ♿

SPALDING TROPICAL FOREST *E7*
AND ROSE COTTAGE WATER GARDEN
CENTRE, GLENSIDE NORTH,
PINCHBECK, NR. SPALDING PE11 3SD
TEL: 01775 710882 FAX: 01775 710882
Signposted 'Tropical Forest' at Pinchbeck

Tropical undercover paradise, with a wonderful display of plants from around the world. **Features:** Tropical house. *Open: All year, Summer 1000-1730; Winter 1000-1600. Closed Christmas, Boxing and New Year's Day £2.45/£1.99/£1.40/£6 (family ticket).* ♿ ♣ 🅿 🆆🅲 🛆 *(Mar-Oct)* 🗙 🗙 *(Mar-Oct)* ☇ *(outside area only)* ♿

❋ **RUTLAND WATER** *(nr. Stamford)* *B/C8/9*
◉ BARNSDALE DROUGHT GARDEN,
BARNSDALE CAR PARK (OFF A606),
RUTLAND WATER, NR. STAMFORD
TEL: 01572 653026 - Rutland Water
Tourist Information Centre
FAX: 01572 653027
Off the A606 at Barnsdale Car Park (Rutland Water).
Created by Anglian Water and the late
Geoff Hamilton, to demonstrate plants and
shrubs which can be grown successfully
without additional watering. **Features:**
Arboretum. **G** - Geoff Hamilton. *Open: All year,
daily (without restrictions), any reasonable time.
Admission free to garden. Car park charge (from £1).*
P **WC** ♨ 🎋 𝕜

❋ **SOUTH SOMERCOTES** *(nr. Louth)* *F3*
THE VILLA, LOUTH ROAD, SOUTH
SOMERCOTES, NR. LOUTH LN11 7BW
TEL: 01507 358487 FAX: 01507 358487
*Eight miles east of Louth on unclassified road,
beyond the village of South Cockerington.*
Small country garden set in peaceful rural
surroundings, and overflowing with interesting
perennials, roses, herbs and shrubs.
Features: Herbaceous borders. Fruit and
vegetable and herb gardens and woodland.
*Open: By appointment only. £1/£1/free (if accompanied
by an adult).* ♨ **P** **WC** ♨ *(by arrangement)* 𝕜

❋ **SPALDING** *E7/8*
◉ AYSCOUGHFEE HALL
MUSEUM & GARDENS,
CHURCHGATE, SPALDING PE11 2RA
TEL: 01775 725468 FAX: 01775 762715
*Turn off A16, between Spalding and Boston.
Into town centre, follow brown signs.*

Medieval wool-merchant's house in five
acres of garden. 17th century Yew Tree
walks, Lutyens war memorial, ice house and
lake. Ideal family venue with a museum in
the Hall, and children's play area, putting
green and tennis courts in the garden.

Features: Herbaceous borders and topiary.
Herb and scent gardens. **G** - William Sands.
*Open: Gardens - all year, daily, 0800 to dusk. Hall
- Mon to Fri, 1000-1700; Sun, 1100-1700. Closed
Winter weekends (Nov-Feb). Admission free.* ⚲ **P**
(limited) **WC** ♨ ✗ *(Apr-Sept only)* 𝕜 🐕 🐈 ♿

❋ **SPALDING** *E7/8*
SPRINGFIELDS GARDENS,
CAMELGATE, SPALDING PE12 6ET
TEL: 01775 724843 FAX: 01775 711209
*One mile east of Spalding town centre, off the
A16 by-pass.*
One of Britain's premier show gardens, with
twenty-five acres of Tulips, Daffodils, Hyacinths,
etc. Plus woodland walk, Palm house,
Carp lake and much more. **Features:**
Herbaceous borders, landscaped parkland
and topiary. Herb, knot, sunken, wildflower
and woodland gardens. *Open: 11 Mar to 7 May,
daily (including Sun), 1000-1800 (last admission
1700). £3/£2.70/free (if accompanied by an adult).*
⚲ ❄ **P** **WC** ♨ 🎋 ✗ 🐈 *(guide dogs only)* ♿
SE - Throughout the year, please contact for
details

❋ **STAMFORD** *C8/9*
◉ BURGHLEY HOUSE,
STAMFORD PE9 3JY
TEL: 01780 752451 FAX: 01780 480125
Clearly signposted from all major routes (including A1).
Sculpture garden in grounds of Elizabethan
stately home, built in 1587 by William Cecil
1st Lord Burghley and Lord Treasurer to
Queen Elizabeth. **Features:** Sculpture
garden, landscaped parkland and statuary/
sculpture, woodland and water garden.
G - Lancelot 'Capability' Brown. *Open: Easter
to early Oct, daily, 1100-1600. Admission free to garden.*
⚲ **P** **WC** ♨ ✗

✤ **THORNTON CURTIS** *(nr. Ulceby)* *C/D1*
THE PALM FARM,
THORNTON HALL GARDENS,
THORNTON CURTIS,
NR. ULCEBY
NORTH LINCOLNSHIRE DN39 6XF
TEL: 01469 531232 FAX: 01469 531232
¹/₄ mile off the A1077. Take Station Road from Thornton Church (6 miles south of Humber Bridge).

Nursery specialising in exotic and unusual trees and shrubs. Explore the garden with its mature plantings of specimen trees, including Hardy Palms and Eucalyptus. **Features:** Palm garden. *Open: All year, daily, 1400-1700 (including Bank Hols). Closed on Sat from Nov-Mar. Admission free.* ✿ ▣ ⚲ ⚲

✤ **WESTON** *(nr. Spalding)* *E7/8*
BAYTREE NURSERIES,
WESTON, NR. SPALDING PE12 6JU
TEL: 01406 370242 FAX: 01406 371665
On the A151 at Weston, just off the new Spalding bypass.

A twenty five acre gardener's paradise, with display gardens, owl centre, children's play area and large pet and aquatic centre. **Features:** Landscaped parkland and statuary/sculpture. Rock/alpine and Rose gardens. *Open: All year, daily, Winter 0900-1730; Summer 0900-1800. Admission free (but charge for owl centre).* ♿ ✿ ▣ ᵂᶜ ⚲ ⚲ ✕ ⚲ ⚲ ⚲

SIR JOSEPH BANKS (1744-1820)

This great botanist and explorer was born in London in 1744. When he was twenty four, he set off with Captain Cook on that first famous voyage of discovery to Australia and the South Pacific. His aim was to collect the many different species of flora, which in turn he introduced back into this country. He became known as one of the founding fathers of Australia. The years following his return saw him become President of the Royal Society and scientific adviser to George III. Banks inherited land at Revesby, Lincolnshire, and purchased a house in the nearby town of Horncastle. There he encouraged better methods of agriculture, and was the greatest planter of trees in the county. You can visit the Sir Joseph Banks Tropical Conservatory in Lincoln.

✤ **WOOLSTHORPE BY COLSTERWORTH** *(nr. Grantham)* *B/C7/8*
WOOLSTHORPE MANOR
(The National Trust), 23 NEWTON WAY,
WOOLSTHORPE BY COLSTERWORTH,
NR. GRANTHAM NG33 5NR
TEL: 01476 860338 FAX: 01476 860338
From A1, follow signs for Woolsthorpe and green National Trust signs.

Woolsthorpe Manor is the family home of the most famous English scientist Isaac Newton. The garden is an orchard, and contains a descendant of the apple tree (Flower of Kent), under which Newton sat and discovered gravity. New science exhibition in 2000. **Features:** Orchard. *Open: Apr to Oct, Wed-Sun, 1300-1700. Also open on Bank Hols £3.20/£1.60/£8.00 (family ticket).* ♿ ▣ ᵂᶜ ⚲ ⚲

✤ **WRAGBY** *D4*
WRAGBY MAZE AND CONIFER CENTRE,
BARDNEY ROAD, WRAGBY LN8 5QZ
TEL: 01673 858660/857372
FAX: 01673 858660
Find us on the B1202, half a mile from the traffic lights in Wragby.

Hedge maze and garden games, including putting, croquet, boules, draughts and tick tack toe. Topiary collection (incl. Wragby Wrabbit). Grower of ornamental and hedging conifers. **Features:** Maze (hedge) and topiary. Conifer and shrub garden. *Open: Maze and gardens – Easter to Nov, daily, 0900-1700. Conifer centre, all year (except Christmas to New Year period), daily, 0900-1700. £1.95/£1.50/75p.* ✿ ▣ ᵂᶜ ⚲ ⚲

Let our great guide take you around the East of England

East of England – The Official Guide 2000

This is a real mine full of information, as great to have to hand at the early stage of your visit to the East of England, as on holiday itself. 164 full colour pages packed with hot tips, facts and figures and plenty of tour ideas. Full details of places to go, thing to see and do, including prices and opening times, plus places to eat, shopping and much much more!

Price: £4.99 (including postage and packing)

This guide is available from the East of England Tourist Board, please telephone (01473) 825624 for further information.

Whether you want to follow the leader - or prefer to stand out from the crowd - with our guides you'll always have your very own local expert to hand.

Garden
DISCOVERY TOURS

Some of the gardens featured within these tours, have limited or restricted opening hours. We have indicated these with an *, and suggest you refer to their entry within this guide (to check opening times), before starting your journey.

BULB LAND
Mix together the home of the British bulb industry and a colourful tropical paradise, and you have this tour based around the peaceful market town of Spalding in Lincolnshire.
Starting point: Spalding *(Lincolnshire)*
Mileage: 3 miles *Morning* – leave Spalding on the road north to the village of Pinchbeck (the old A16) to visit The Spalding Bulb Museum, where you can learn about the history of the industry. Then visit the steamy Tropical Forest, before returning to Spalding.
Afternoon – visit the colourful gardens of Ayscoughfee Hall, Museum & Garden, then end the day at the famous 'bulb' showground of Springfields, with its Daffodils, Hyacinths and Tulips.

SECRET GARDENS OF CAMBRIDGESHIRE
The oldest continually inhabited house, a wonderful medieval garden and a spectacular collection of roses – 'Open the door' on the secret gardens of Cambridgeshire.
Starting point: Huntingdon *(Cambridgeshire)*
Mileage: 39 miles *Morning* – leave Huntingdon on the A1123 to St. Ives, where you take the B1040 south towards Hilton. Half a mile after leaving the town, turn right to Hemingford Grey to visit The Manor, the oldest continually inhabited house in England. After your visit, retrace your steps to the B1040 and turn right. One mile later, at the junction with the A14, turn right again and follow this northwards (it shortly becomes the A1) towards Peterborough.

Afternoon – after about twenty seven miles, you reach the junction with the A47. Leave the A1 here, and follow signs into the village of Wansford. In the centre, take the unclassified road south through Yarwell, to the village of Nassington. Visit the medieval garden at *Prebendal Manor, then take the unclassified road south towards Fotheringay. After about a mile turn left to the village of Elton, where you can take a walk amongst the Roses at Elton Hall.

GARDENS OF THE WORLD
From the traditional English knot garden and pagodas of Japan, to the tropical climates of Australia and South America – explore the gardens of the world.
Starting point: Lincoln *(Lincolnshire)*
Mileage: 18 miles *Morning* – start the day in the city by visiting The Lawn, where you can enjoy the tropical Sir Joseph Banks Conservatory and adjoining John Dawber Garden. After your visit, leave Lincoln on the A57 towards Worksop. After ten miles, turn left onto the A1133 south to North Clifton.
Afternoon – visit the pagodas and waterfalls of the Pureland 'Japanese Garden', then retrace your steps along the A1133 to the junction with the A57. Turn right back towards Lincoln. About three miles later, turn right onto the B1190 to Doddington. End the day at the Elizabethan *Doddington Hall & Gardens with its traditionally 'English' garden.

TOWN AND COUNTRY
Enjoy the bustling 'garden city' of Cambridge, with its green open spaces and riverside meadows, then it's into the countryside, to the outstanding hundred acre garden of Anglesey Abbey.
Starting point: Cambridge *(Cambridgeshire)*
Mileage: 5 miles *Morning* – start the day in Cambridge, visit the Botanic Garden and try your hand at punting. *Afternoon* – leave Cambridge on the A1303 towards Newmarket. At the junction with the A14, take the B1102 towards Burwell, following the brown and white signs to Anglesey Abbey, Gardens and Lode Mill. Visit this 17th century house and its outstanding garden.

RESTORING THE PAST

Discover the historical treasures of Lincolnshire, on this tour of gardens and houses which have been restored to their former glory.

Starting point: Stamford (Lincolnshire)
Mileage: 35 miles
Morning - take the A1 north towards Grantham. After about six miles, turn right onto an unclassified road to Clipsham. Visit the unusual Yew Tree Avenue with its bizarrely clipped trees. Continue along the unclassified road to Little Bytham. Here you join the B1176 north to Corby Glen. At the junction with the A151, turn right to Grimsthorpe. Visit the magnificent castle gardens with their wildflowers, Roses and vegetable garden. *Afternoon* - after lunch, return along the A151 to Corby Glen. Then head north to Grantham on the B1176/A52. Leave the town on the A607 north to Belton. End the day within the pleasure gardens and grounds of Belton House.

Peckover House, Cambridgeshire

Gunby Hall, Lincolnshire

AN ENGLISH COUNTRY GARDEN

Enjoy the pleasures of traditional English country gardens on this tour. From awarding-winning Geraniums and rambling Roses, to healing herbs and Tennyson's reputed 'haunt of ancient peace'.

Starting point: Spilsby (Lincolnshire)
Mileage: 7 miles. *Morning* - start the day within the cottage garden of Choice Plants. Enjoy the special collection of Hardy Geraniums. Then head north along the A16 to the roundabout with the A158. Turn right to the village of Candlesby. Visit the specialist herb workshop and nursery. *Afternoon* - continue along the A158 for a further mile to visit Tennyson's 'haunt of ancient peace', the red-brick Gunby Hall, with its English vegetables, fruits and flowers.

A TASTE OF PARADISE –
Butterflies, Beer and Borders

From a tropical world of colourful butter-flies, and a 'real ale' brewery garden, to the fruity passions of Peckover House – enjoy three very distinctive gardens.

Starting point: Long Sutton *(Lincolnshire)*
Mileage: 7 miles. *Morning* – visit The Butterfly & Wildlife Park, where tropical butterflies land right in your hands. *Afternoon* – leave the town of Long Sutton on the A1101 south to Wisbech. Begin with a visit to the Elgood's Brewery Gardens with its unusual trees. Then end the day at the Georgian Peckover House & Garden, and discover its orangery and fernery.

Elgood's Brewery Gardens, Cambridgeshire

MAP OF CAMBRIDGESHIRE & LINCOLNSHIRE

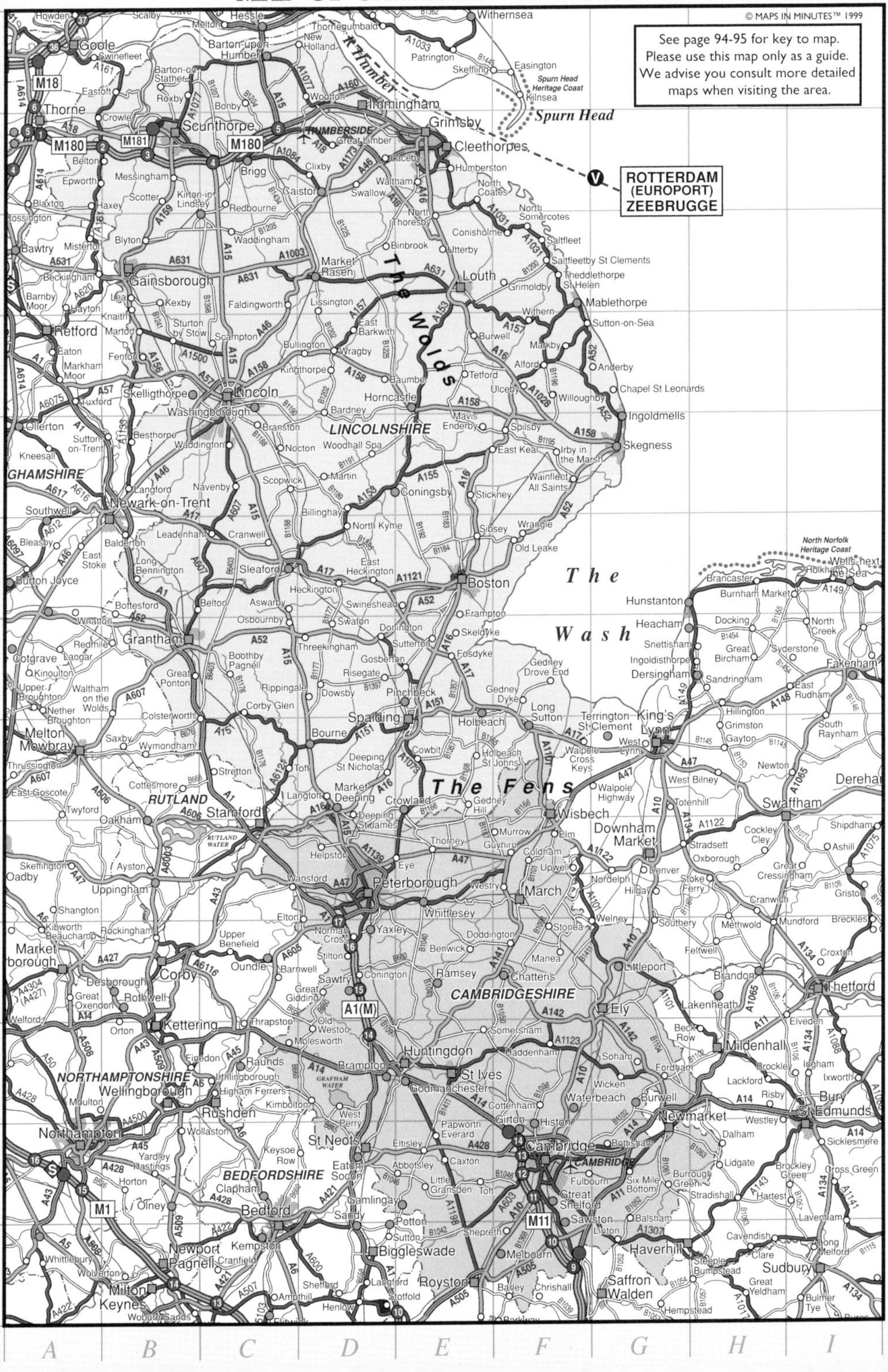

See page 94-95 for key to map.
Please use this map only as a guide.
We advise you consult more detailed
maps when visiting the area.

ROTTERDAM (EUROPORT) ZEEBRUGGE

Spurn Head
Spurn Head Heritage Coast

LINCOLNSHIRE

The Wolds

The Wash

The Fens

CAMBRIDGESHIRE

RUTLAND

NORTHAMPTONSHIRE

BEDFORDSHIRE

North Norfolk Heritage Coast

Selected place names visible on map: Goole, Scunthorpe, Grimsby, Cleethorpes, Brigg, Gainsborough, Louth, Mablethorpe, Lincoln, Horncastle, Skegness, Newark-on-Trent, Grantham, Boston, Hunstanton, Fakenham, Spalding, King's Lynn, Swaffham, Melton Mowbray, Stamford, Oakham, Peterborough, Wisbech, Downham Market, March, Thetford, Uppingham, Kettering, Corby, Huntingdon, Ely, Mildenhall, Bury St Edmunds, Northampton, Wellingborough, Rushden, St Neots, Cambridge, Newmarket, Milton Keynes, Bedford, Biggleswade, Royston, Saffron Walden, Haverhill, Sudbury

Adrian Bloom, *Bressingham Gardens*
(BRESSINGHAM, NR. DISS, NORFOLK)

"Norfolk and Suffolk maybe on the way to nowhere, but this pleasant, largely unspoilt countryside has considerable horticultural attractions. Large and small, old and new, gardens are too numerous to mention. Specialist collections and nurseries, in Roses, Clematis, Lavenders – even Bamboos and Hostas are there to be discovered. At Bressingham, right on the borders of the two counties are two gardens with one of the largest collections of perennials and Conifers in the world. Why not come to Norfolk and Suffolk and take some lasting memories away with you?"

ADRIAN'S FAVOURITE THREE PLANTS:
Hakonechloa macra albo aurea (a great ornamental grass), Snowdrop (Galanthus – harbinger of Spring), Hamamelis (the Witch Hazel with winter fragrance)

ADRIAN'S GARDENING HINT:
"When does a potential garden asset become a liability?"

"If you buy the fastest growing conifer for a hedge (Cuppressocyparis Leylandii) and forget to trim it!

You can visit gardens galore in Norfolk and Suffolk – from charming cottage gardens on village open days to the sweeping splendours of Royal Sandringham and a whole court of stately homes. Stroll through a carefully-tended riot of colour in seafront gardens like those at Hunstanton, Cromer, Lowestoft and Felixstowe. Or stride through the gorse and heather in the wild heathland of Dunwich on the Suffolk coast. Water gardens, arboretums, vineyards, herb gardens, there's a feast for the senses wherever you go from old fashioned Rose gardens to fields of purple Lavender.

That Georgian charmer, Bury St Edmunds, makes the perfect base for exploring Suffolk's horticultural delights. As the 1999 winner of "Britain in Bloom", it prides itself on its floral displays from window boxes and hanging baskets to the spectacular Abbey Gardens.

Ramble with the roses in cosseted cottage gardens in the picture book villages of Chelsworth, Eye and Walsham-le-Willows at Garden Festival time. If you prefer your gardens on a grander scale, the National Trust have some splendid specimens. Nearby Ickworth House boasts an elegant Italianate Garden and a lovely scented walk. While up in Norfolk, Felbrigg Hall, Blickling Hall and Oxburgh Hall are each worth a day's visit for their impressive walled gardens and magnificent parks and woodland walks. Sheringham Park, famed for its Rhododendrons and spectacular views over coast and countryside, was designed by Humphry Repton, the famous landscape designer. Admire his work, and then visit his tomb at nearby Aylsham Church.

A short walk from Sheringham Park takes you to the North Norfolk Steam Railway, the Poppy Line as it came to be called after this beautiful stretch of the Norfolk coast was "discovered" by fashionable turn of the century artists and actors. You can mix beautiful scenery and steam at Bressingham too, where

Alan and Adrian Bloom have created superb gardens and nurseries and the most impressive collection of old steam machines from railway to traction engines and even a Victorian carousel.

The scent of Lavender and Roses also conjure up scenes of old world England. Revel in the fields of mauve and purple of Norfolk Lavender and in the gorgeous Rose gardens at Elsing Hall, Helmingham Hall and Mannington Hall, as well as at Peter Beales Classic Collection at Attleborough. There are more treats in store at some fascinating herb gardens at Castle Acre Priory, Congham Hall, Bruisyard and Norfolk Herbs.

Exotic species from faraway places have settled happily at the African Violet Centre, the Eau Brink Cacti Desert Plant Collection and at the Lynford Arboretum in Thetford Forest.

Take a vintage boat trip from the water gardens of the Fairhaven Garden Trust and explore the other lush and lovely gardens of the Norfolk Broads, like Hoveton Hall and East Ruston Old Vicarage. Somerleyton Hall is another 'must'. But leave plenty of time to find your way out of the famous yew maze.

And when you've visited all these, don't you deserve a relaxing glass of wine? Well, there are more than a dozen vineyards to visit. Good health and good gardening!

On the following pages you will find information about many of the region's gardens, including contact details, directions, special features and facilities available. Shown below is a key to the symbols used on the entries. A map reference has been provided; to be used with the map on page 68. Prices shown are Adults/OAP's/Children. We do advise that you contact the individual gardens before visiting, to check opening times and admission prices, as changes do occur after press date.

Helmingham Hall, Suffolk

KEY TO SYMBOLS

- ⊛ Member of the East of England Tourist Board
- ⊞ gift shop
- ⚘ plants/produce for sale
- 🅿 parking
- [wc] toilet facilities
- ⚱ light refreshments/snacks
- 🅰 picnic area
- ✕ restaurant/tearoom
- 𝑗 pre-booked guided tours/talks
- 🐕 dogs permitted on lead
- ♿ disabled visitors welcome
- SE special events
- 🅖 connection to famous gardener

45

✤ **ATTLEBOROUGH** *E6*
◉ PETER BEALES CLASSIC ROSE
GARDENS, LONDON ROAD,
ATTLEBOROUGH NR17 1AY
TEL: 01953 454707 FAX: 01953 456845
Email: sales@classicroses.co.uk
www.classicroses.co.uk
*Leave the A11 at the Breckland Lodge - the
entrance to the gardens is within 500 yards.*

Two and a half acres of beautiful Rose
gardens, featuring the majority of Peter
Beales world famous collection. **Features:**
Rose garden. National Collection of Rosa
(species). 🄶 - Peter Beales. *Open: Summer
months - weekdays, Sun and Bank Hols, 1000-
1600. Admission free.* ✿ 🅿 ᵂᶜ ᴀ 🏹 🐾 ᴣ

✤ **BEESTON REGIS** *(nr. Sheringham)* F2/3
PRIORY MAZE & GARDENS,
CROMER ROAD, BEESTON REGIS,
NR. SHERINGHAM NR26 8SF
TEL: 01263 822986 FAX: 01263 822986
One mile east of Sheringham on the A149.

Beech hedge maze, Christmas tree maze,
wildflower meadow, ponds and stream.
Demonstration flower beds and woodland
walks, all within a ten acre landscape.
Features: Herbaceous borders,
landscaped parkland, maze (hedge,
Christmas tree) and statuary/sculpture.
Wildflower and woodland gardens. *Open: Jun
to mid Sept, Tues-Fri and Sun, 1000-1700.
£2.80/£2.80/£1.40* ✿ 🅿 ᵂᶜ ᴀ 🏹

✤ **BLICKLING** *(nr. Norwich)* F3
◉ BLICKLING HALL, PARK & GARDEN
(The National Trust), BLICKLING,
NR. NORWICH NR11 6NF
TEL: 01263 738030 FAX: 01263 731660
*Fifteen miles north of Norwich. On north side of
B1354, one and a quarter miles northwest of
Aylsham on the A140.*

Magnificent Jacobean mansion with colourful
large garden, including parterre and
herbaceous borders. Secret garden with
summer house and scented plants. 18th

century temple and Orangery. Formal
woodland wilderness garden. Famous mature
Yew hedging and topiary. Dry moat. Beautiful
park and lakeside walks. Adjacent plant
centre. **Features:** Garden folly, herbaceous
borders, landscaped parkland, statuary/
sculpture, topiary and tropical house. Dell,
parterre, scent, sunken, wildflower and
woodland gardens. 🄶 - Norah Lyndsey. *Open:
8 Apr to 29 Oct, daily except Mon and Tues (open
Bank Hol Mon) Tues-Sun in Aug, 1300-1630.
Garden: 8 Apr to 29 Oct, as house, Tues-Sun in
Aug, 1030-1730. 2 Nov-17 Dec, Thur-Sun,
6 Jan-Mar 2001, Sat-Sun, 1100-1600. House &
Garden: £6.50/£6.50/£3.60 Garden only: £3.70/
£3.70/£1.75* ♿✿🅿 ᵂᶜ ᴀ 🏹 ✗ 🍴 🐾 *(not in gardens)*
& SE - Blickling celebrates 60 years of NT
protection with a special events programme,
phone for details.

✤ **BRADENHAM** *(nr. East Dereham)* D5
BRADENHAM HALL GARDENS
AND ARBORETUM,
BRADENHAM, THETFORD IP25 7QP
TEL: 01362 687243 FAX: 01362 687669
*Off the A47 - eight miles east of Swaffham, five
miles west of Dereham*

A garden for all seasons, including arboretum
with over 1,000 species, all labelled.
Herbaceous shrubs, mixed borders, old-
fashioned Roses, wall shrubs and climbers.
Features: Arboretum, garden folly,
herbaceous borders, landscaped parkland
and statuary/sculpture. Fruit and vegetable,
herb, Italian, kitchen, Rose and woodland
gardens Special collection of Daffodils
(eighty varieties) in named groups. *Open:
Apr to Sept, 2nd, 4th and 5th Suns of the month,
1400-1730. £3/£3/free. Groups by appointment*
✿ 🅿 ᵂᶜ ᴀ ✗ &

✤ **BRESSINGHAM** *(nr. Diss)* E7
◉ BRESSINGHAM GARDENS
BRESSINGHAM, NR. DISS IP22 2AB
TEL: 01379 688402 FAX: 01379 687788
*Three miles west of Diss on the A1066 (Diss to
Thetford road).*

Two separate world renowned six acre
gardens. Alan Bloom's Dell Garden - forty
seven island beds in attractive setting,
containing nearly 5,000 species and varieties
of hardy perennials. Adrian Bloom's 'Foggy
Bottom' garden - Conifers and trees provide
a colourful background structure to a wide
variety of plants, vistas and plant associations
for every season. This is a private garden
within walking distance of the Dell garden.
Features: Island beds, year round ('Foggy
Bottom') and Conifer gardens. Special

cont.

collections of Hardy Geraniums and Crocosmias (Dell Garden), Conifers and Ornamental Grasses ('Foggy Bottom' garden). Wide variety of Bressingham speciality plants on sale at the newly refurbished plant centre. Dell Garden. 🄶 - Alan and Adrian Bloom. *Open: Dell Garden (and adjoining Steam Museum) - 1 Apr to 31 Oct, daily, 1030-1700. 'Foggy Bottom' garden - admission charges to Dell Garden. £3/£2.50/free. Admission separate to 'Foggy Bottom' garden - £3/£2.50/free.* 🚾 🌼 *(plant centre)* 🅿 🆆🅲 ♨ 🍴 ✕ 🎠 ♿ SE - 4, 5 Mar.

※ **CASTLE ACRE** *(nr. King's Lynn)* C4
❀ CASTLE ACRE PRIORY
(English Heritage), STOCKS GREEN,
CASTLE ACRE,
NR. KING'S LYNN PE32 2XD
TEL: 01760 755394 FAX: 01760 755594
Off the B1065 (Swaffham to Fakenham road). Turn off towards Castle Acre.

Remains of a Cluniac Priory. There is a modern representation of a medieval herb garden, laid out in culinary, medicinal, decorative and strewing sections. **Features:** Herb and scent gardens. *Open: 1 Apr to 30 Sept, 1000-1800, daily. 1 Oct to 31 Oct, 1000-1700, daily. 1 Nov - 31 Mar 2001, 1000-1600 Wed - Sun. Closed 24-26 Dec and 1 Jan 2001. £3.20/£2.40/£1.60.* 🚾 🅿 🆆🅲 ♨ 🍴 🐕 ♿

※ **EAST HARLING** *(nr. Norwich)* D/E6
❀ HARLING VINEYARDS,
EASTFIELD HOUSE, CHURCH ROAD,
EAST HARLING, NR. NORWICH
NR16 2NA TEL: 01953 717341
Two miles from A11, on B1111 (east of Thetford).

Established and diverse nine acre garden, set around a Victorian mansion and beside an imposing church. Large mature vineyard. Grounds lead down to river. **Features:** Herbaceous borders, statuary/sculpture and vineyard. Fruit and vegetable, herb and rock/alpine gardens. *Open: Good Fri to Oct, daily from 1030 (last admission 1800). Other times by appointment £2.50/£2.50/free (if accompanied by an adult). Admission may be discounted for wine purchasers.* 🚾 🌼 🅿 🆆🅲 🎠 🐕 ♿

※ **EAST RUSTON** *(nr. Norwich)* G3/4
❀ EAST RUSTON OLD VICARAGE
GARDEN, EAST RUSTON,
NR. NORWICH NR12 9HN
TEL: 01603 632350 FAX: 01692 650233
Turn off A149 (signposted Bacton and Happisburgh). Ignore signs to East Ruston, garden next to East Ruston church.

A remarkable fourteen acre exotic garden including Mediterranean, kitchen and sunken gardens. Tropical and autumn borders with wildflower meadows, all varying strongly in mood. A feast of formal design, decorative exuberance and brilliant planting. Lavish pots and finely detailed gates play their decorative part. Many unusual plants for sale. **Features:** Garden pavilions & summerhouse, herbaceous borders, statuary/sculpture, topiary and tropical house. Dutch, fruit and vegetable, cutting, mediterranean, parterre, sunken and wild-flower gardens. Special collections of Canna, Dahlia, Banana and Hydrangea. *Open: 23 Apr to 29 Oct, Sun, Wed, Fri and Bank Hols, 1400-1730. £3.50/£3.50/£1.* 🌼 🅿 🆆🅲 🍴 ♨ ✕ 🎠 ♿

※ **EAU BRINK**
(nr. King's Lynn) B4
EAU BRINK CACTI,
EAU BRINK ROAD, TILNEY ALL SAINTS,
NR. KING'S LYNN PE34 4SQ
TEL: 01553 617635
First turning left from West Lynn roundabout, on the A47 to Wisbech.

A large collection of Cacti and Succulents, displayed in quarter of an acre of green houses. *Open: Mar to Oct, Sun to Thurs 1000-1700. Nov to Feb 1100-1500. Admission free.* 🌼 🅿 🆆🅲 🍴 🎠

✤ **ELSING** *(nr. Dereham)* E4
ELSING HALL, ELSING,
NR. DEREHAM NR20 3DX
TEL: 01362 637224 FAX: 01362 637224

Take A47 to Dereham, then B1110 to North Tuddenham - follow signs.

Moated historic house, setting for masses of old fashioned Roses, allowed to ramble naturally up walls and trees. Plus eight acres of interesting features and plants. **Features:** Arboretum, garden folly (arches), landscaped parkland, statuary/ sculpture and topiary. Rose, scent, water, wildflower and woodland gardens. *Open: Jun to Sept, Sun, 1400-1800. £3/£3/free.* ✿ 🅿 🆆 🎋 🐾 ♿

✤ **ERPINGHAM** *(nr. Norwich)* F3
◎ ALBY CRAFTS AND GARDENS,
ERPINGHAM, NR. NORWICH NR11 7QE
TEL: 01263 761226 FAX: 01263 768811
On the A140 between Aylsham and Cromer.

Four acres of gardens and ponds. Specialising in unusual shrubs, plants and bulbs. **Features:** Herbaceous borders and landscaped grassland. Bog and wildflower gardens. *Open: Mid Mar to end Oct, Tues-Sun, 1000-1700. £2/£2/free.* ♿ 🅿 🆆 ✕ 🎋 ♿ SE - throughout year, please telephone for details.

✤ **EUSTON** *(nr. Thetford)* D7
◎ EUSTON HALL AND GARDEN,
C/O ESTATE OFFICE, EUSTON,
NR. THETFORD IP24 2QP
On A1088, twelve miles north of Bury St. Edmunds.

Historic 'Pleasure Grounds' designed by John Evelyn and William Kent. Lake and river walk to watermill. Herbaceous borders and rose gardens. **Features:** Garden folly, herbaceous borders and landscaped parkland. Rose garden. 🅖 - Lancelot 'Capability' Brown, John Evelyn and William Kent. *Open: 1 Jun to 28 Sept, Thurs, 1430-1700. Suns - 25 Jun; 3 Sept, 1430-1700. Gardens £1/£1/50p. House and gardens - £3/£2.50.* ♿ 🅿 🆆 🎋 ✕ ♿ *(garden only)* SE - 21 May.

✤ **FAKENHAM** D3
◎ PENSTHORPE WATERFOWL PARK,
FAKENHAM NR21 0LN
TEL: 01328 851465 FAX: 01328 855905
Clearly signposted off the A1067 (Norwich to Fakenham road).

200 acres of superb park and wetland nature reserve, with exotic and other waterfowl. Enjoy wildflower meadows and woodland walks. Most paths suitable for elderly and disabled. An acre of recently planted perennial garden, designed by Piet Oudolf. **Features:** Herbaceous borders, water and butterfly garden. *Open: Spring, Summer and Autumn, daily, 1000-1700. Winter (Jan, Feb and Mar), weekends only, 1000-1700. £4.50/£4/£2.* ♿ 🅿 🆆 ⚓ 🎋 ✕ 🎋 ♿ SE - 3, 4 Jun

✤ **FILBY** *(nr. Great Yarmouth)* H4/5
◎ THRIGBY HALL
WILDLIFE GARDENS, FILBY,
NR. GREAT YARMOUTH NR29 3DR
TEL: 01493 369477 FAX: 01493 368256
South of Filby - off the A1064 (Acle to Caister road).

A special collection of Asian animals in the 270 year old landscaped grounds and gardens of Thrigby Hall. Tree walk. **Features:** Garden folly (willow pattern bridge) and tropical house. Chinese garden. *Open: All year, daily from 1000. £5.50/£4.90/£3.90.* ♿ 🅿 🆆 ⚓ 🎋 ♿

✤ **FRITTON** *(nr. Great Yarmouth)* H5
◎ FRITTON LAKE, FRITTON,
NR. GREAT YARMOUTH NR31 9HA
TEL: 01493 488288 FAX: 01493 488355
Off the A143 (Beccles to Great Yarmouth road), at eastern end of Fritton village.

Country park with beautiful lakeside gardens, including formal Victorian walled garden and woodland garden with wildflowers. Also lost gardens of Fritton Hall with Rhododendrons, Azaleas, old terraces and avenue, set in a woodland setting. Two mile lake with boating

and launch trips, falconry centre, heavy horse stables and nine hole golf course. **Features:** Herbaceous borders and landscaped parkland. Woodland garden. *Open: 1 Apr to end Sept, daily, 1000-1730. Oct weekends, £5.20/£4.80/£3.80 (discounts for groups).* ⚲ P ᴡᴄ 🚻 Å ✕ ⚹ ♿

✤ **GOODERSTONE** *(nr. King's Lynn)*   C5
GOODERSTONE WATER GARDENS,
GOODERSTONE,
NR. KING'S LYNN PE33 9DA
TEL: 01366 328646
Six miles south-west of Swaffham, off the A1065 towards Oxborough.

Delightful landscaped water gardens with flowers, shrubs, grassy walks, lake, pools and bridges. Herbaceous plants, Roses and woodland walk. **Features:** Water garden. *Open: Apr to (2nd week) of Oct, daily, 1030-1730. £1.50/£1.50/50p.* ᴡᴄ Å

✤ **GREAT ELLINGHAM** *(nr. Attleborough)* E6
◎ TROPICAL BUTTERFLY GARDENS
AND BIRD PARK, GREAT ELLINGHAM,
NR. ATTLEBOROUGH NR17 1AW
TEL: 01953 453175 FAX: 01953 453175
Signposted from the A11 (Attleborough bypass), and the B1077 (Watton road).

Enclosed tropical gardens, with free-flying butterflies and birds. Also fifteen acre waterside walk, falconry centre and two acre garden centre. **Features:** Landscaped parkland and tropical house. Water, wild-flower and woodland gardens. *Open: Mar to Oct, Mon-Sat, 0900-1730; Sun and Bank Hols, 1000-1730. £3.45/£3.25/£1.95.* ⚲ ⚹ P ᴡᴄ 🚻 Å ✕ ⚹ 🐦 *(in some areas)* ♿

✤ **GRESSENHALL** *(nr. Dereham)*

◎ GRESSENHALL NORFOLK   D4
RURAL LIFE MUSEUM
BEECH HOUSE, GRESSENHALL,
NR. DEREHAM NR20 4DR
TEL: 01362 860563 FAX: 01362 860385
Three miles north-west of East Dereham, on the B1146 at Gressenhall.

Award-winning museum and farm, featuring Edwardian "Cherry Tree Cottage Garden". Wildlife garden, wildflower meadow and traditional Norfolk apple orchard, and farm-house demonstration garden. **Features:** Norfolk varieties of apples and 1912 fruit and vegetables. *Open: 1 Apr to 29 Oct, daily, 1000-1700, £3.90/£2.90/£1.80.* ⚲ ⚹ P ᴡᴄ 🚻 Å ✕ ⚹ ♿

◎ NORFOLK HERBS,   D4
BLACKBERRY FARM, DILLINGTON,
NR. GRESSENHALL
DEREHAM NR19 2QD
TEL: 01362 860812 FAX: 01362 860812
Take B1110 north from Dereham, first left to Dillington, nursery is one and a half miles on right.

Norfolk's specialist herb nursery, set in a beautiful wooded valley renowned for its wildlife. Visitors can enjoy the herb garden and surrounding meadowland, or choose from a vast array of culinary, medicinal and aromatic herb plants, and hand thrown terracotta. Advice and information available on all aspects of herb growing. **Features:** Herb garden and wildflower meadow. *Open: Apr to Jul, daily, 0900-1800. Aug, Tues-Sun, 0900-1800. Sept to Mar, Wed-Sat, 0900-1700. Closed Christmas to end Jan. Admission free.* ⚹ P ᴡᴄ Å ⚹ 🐦 ♿

✣ **GRIMSTON** *(nr. King's Lynn)* C4
◉ CONGHAM HALL HERB GARDENS, LYNN ROAD, GRIMSTON, NR. KING'S LYNN PE32 1AH
TEL: 01485 600250 FAX: 01485 601191
From A149/A148 interchange (north-east of King's Lynn), follow A148 towards Fakenham and Cromer for 100yds. Then turn right to Grimston - hotel is two and a half miles on left.

A collection of approximately 700 labelled herbs in formal and casual layouts. Potager, wild flower garden and vegetables grown for use in the adjacent hotel. **Features:** Herb garden. *Open: Apr to Sept, Sun-Fri, 1400-1600. Admission free.* ✣ 🅿 🆆

✣ **HEACHAM** B3
◉ NORFOLK LAVENDER LIMITED, CALEY MILL, HEACHAM PE31 7JE
TEL: 01485 570384 FAX: 01485 571176
Situated beside A149 (King's Lynn to Hunstanton road) at Heacham.

Six acres of all year fragrance to explore, including herb garden, Lavenders and a fragrant meadow garden with shrubs, Mediterranean and waterside plants. Fragrant plant centre. **Features:** Herbaceous borders. Herb and scented gardens. National Collection of Lavandula. *Open: All year, daily, 0900-1700 (except 25, 26 Dec and 1 Jan). Admission free.* ⬛ ✣ 🅿 🆆 🍴 ✕ 🎇 🐾 ♿

✣ **HOLKHAM** *(nr. Wells next the Sea)* D2

◉ HOLKHAM HALL, HOLKHAM, NR. WELLS-NEXT-THE-SEA NR23 1AB
TEL: 01328 710227 FAX: 01328 711707
Two miles west of Wells-next-the-Sea.

Holkham is one of Britain's most majestic stately homes, situated in a beautiful 3,000 acre deer park on the North Norfolk coast. **Features:** Landscaped parkland. *Open: 28 May to 28 Sept, Sun-Thurs, 1300-1700. Also Easter, May and Summer Bank Hols, Sun and Mon, 1130-1700. Hall and museum - £6/£6/£3. Hall or museum - £4/£4/£2.* ⬛ ✣ 🅿 🆆 🍴 🎇 ✕ 🎇 🐾

◉ HOLKHAM NURSERY GARDENS, D2
HOLKHAM, NR. WELLS-NEXT-THE-SEA NR23 1AB
TEL: 01328 711636 FAX: 01328 711117
Entrance through Holkham Park from A149, or from B1155 - follow signs.

Long-established nursery raising own wide selection of shrubs, herbaceous perennials,

climbers and alpines, in splendid 18th century, former walled kitchen garden of Holkham Hall. **Features:** Herbaceous borders. Former kitchen garden, walled garden. Special collection of Lavender. 🅖 - Samuel Wyatt. *Open: All year, daily, 1000-1700 (or dusk if earlier). Closed Christmas and Boxing Day. Admission free (but charge for children £5).* ✣ 🅿 🍴 🐾 ♿

✣ **HOLT** E3
◉ NATURAL SURROUNDINGS, BAYFIELD ESTATE, HOLT NR25 7JN
TEL: 01263 711091
Near Glandford, on the Letheringsett to Blakeney road - off the A148.

A wildflower centre set in the Glaven Valley area of outstanding natural beauty, on the historic Bayfield Estate. Ten acres of gardens and trails. **Features:** Fruit and vegetable, herb, woodland and wildflower gardens. *Open: Summer - Tues-Sun, 1000-1730; Winter - Thurs-Sun, 1000-1600. £1.95/£1.50/£1.* ⬛ ✣ 🅿 🆆 🍴 🎇 🎇 SE - Throughout the year.

✣ **HOUGHTON** *(nr. King's Lynn)* C3
◉ HOUGHTON HALL, HOUGHTON, NR. KING'S LYNN PE31 6UE
TEL: 01485 528569 FAX: 01485 528167
Signposted off the A148 between Fakenham (ten miles), and King's Lynn (fourteen miles).

18th century Palladian mansion built by Sir Robert Walpole. Collection of 20,000 model soldiers. Situated in beautiful parkland, with newly restored walled garden. Wildflower meadows. **Features:** Herbaceous borders, landscaped parkland and statuary/sculpture. Fruit and vegetable, herb, parterre, Rose, wildflower and woodland gardens. 🅖 - Charles Bridgeman. *Open: Easter Sun to the last Sun in Sept, Thurs, Sun and Bank Hol Mon, 1400-1730 (last admission 1700). £6/£6/£3.* ⬛ ✣ 🅿 🆆 🍴 🎇 ✕ ♿

✣ **HOVETON** *(nr. Norwich)* G4
◉ HOVETON HALL GARDENS, HOVETON, NR. NORWICH NR12 8RJ
TEL: 01603 782798 FAX: 01603 784564
Follow brown and white tourist signs off A1151, just north of Wroxham.

Ten acres of Rhododendron and Azalea filled woodlands, laced with streams and leading to a lake. Daffodils galore in Spring. Formal walled, herbaceous and vegetable gardens. Plant sales available beside the tearooms. Light lunches and homemade afternoon teas served in the Old 'Milking Parlour'. **Features:** Famous 'spider'

walled garden. Rhododendrons and Azaleas. *Open: Sun 9 & 16 Apr, Easter Sun to mid Sept, Wed, Fri, Sun and Bank Hol Mon, 1100-1730. £3/£3/£1 (5-14yrs).* ✿ P WC ♿ ⇟ ✕ ⋔ ♿

✤ HUNTANTON B3
◎ ESPLANADE GARDENS, CLIFF PARADE, HUNSTANTON
TEL: 01485 532610 - Hunstanton Tourist Information Centre
FAX: 01485 533972
In the town centre, adjacent to the Green.

Beautifully maintained by the Borough Council of King's Lynn and West Norfolk, the peaceful Esplanade Gardens provide a blaze of colour in Spring and Summer. *Open: All year, daily, any reasonable time. Admission free.* WC ⇟ ⇟ ⋔ ♿

✤ KING'S LYNN B4
◎ THE WALKS, ST. JAMES ROAD/ TENNYSON ROAD, KING'S LYNN
TEL: 01553 763044 - King's Lynn Tourist Information Centre FAX: 01553 777281
In the centre of King's Lynn, near the railway station.

A large, open park in the heart of King's Lynn, cross-cut with tree-lined avenues. Bandstand, ponds, tennis courts and the 15th century 'Red Mount Chapel'. *Open: All year, daily, any reasonable time. Admission free.* ⇟ ⋔ ♿

✤ LODDON G5/6
HALES HALL GARDEN AND HISTORIC BARN, HALES HALL, LODDON NR14 6QW TEL: 01508 548395
Signposted 'Hales Hall' on the A146 - two miles south of Loddon.

Garden with topiary, borders, lawns, Tudor courtyard and moat, rose and fruit gardens. Scented shrubs and climbers in setting of medieval brick buildings, including Great Barn (circa.1485). **Features:** Topiary and tropical house. Herbaceous borders. Rose garden. National Collections of Citrus, Ficus (figs) and Vitis vinifera (grapes). Special collection of Bougainvilleas. *Open: Easter to Oct, Tues-Sat, 1000-1700; Sun and Bank Hol Mon, 1100-1600. Closed Good Fri and 25 Dec-6 Jan. £1.50/£1.50/free (if accompanied by an adult).* ✿ P WC ⇟ ♿ SE - garden workshops during year

LAVENDER COUNTRY
The county of Norfolk is the home of English Lavender, a fragrant plant whose uses seem never-ending, from sweet-smelling pot-pourri and soap, to refreshing Lavender water. The Romans probably brought it to Britain, aware as they were of its many uses for things like first aid, massage oil and insect repellent. Its name comes from the Latin word 'lavandum' which translates as 'fit for washing'. During medieval times, monasteries used Lavender in their medical remedies and by the 16th century, it was used in every room of the house – for everything from an air freshener to a tooth cleaner! In the 17th century, Lavender oil was first used in soap and during the Great Plague of 1665, it was burnt to cleanse the air. But Lavender is probably most associated with the Victorian period, when it became highly fashionable through its use in perfumery and the scenting of linen and clothes. After the First World War, there was a decline in commercial Lavender growing, and although small plots are still grown, the largest full-scale Lavender farm is run by Norfolk Lavender Limited. It was here in 1932, that local nurseryman Linn Chilvers planted six acres of lavender and harvested the first crop a year later. Today, you can visit the home of Norfolk Lavender at Heacham, where there are perfumed gardens of Lavender, including the National Collection.

✤ **MUNDFORD** *(nr. Thetford)* C6

◉ LYNFORD ARBORETUM,
MUNDFORD, NR. THETFORD
TEL: 01842 810271 - Forestry
Commission FAX: 01842 811309
Signposted from the A1065, eight miles north of Brandon.

The arboretum contains over 200 species of Conifers and broad leaves, both in plots and as individual specimens. Pleasant walks around the adjacent Lynford Lakes. **Features:** Arboretum. *Open: All year, daily, any reasonable time. Admission free.* 🅿 🎋 ⚏

'MAGPIES' GARDEN AND UNUSUAL HARDY PLANT NURSERY,
'MAGPIES', GREEN LANE,
MUNDFORD, NR.THETFORD IP26 5HS
TEL: 01842 878496
Take A1065 from Mundford towards Swaffham. After quarter of a mile, turn left into Green Lane.

Intensively planted in the cottage garden style, this is a garden to get lost in! Featured in several magazines. Adjoining nursery. **Features:** Arboretum, garden folly (gazebo), herbaceous borders and statuary/ sculpture. Fruit and vegetable, kitchen, rock/alpine and woodland gardens. *Open: Spring to Autumn, Mon-Fri, 0900-1700 (closed Wed); Sat and Sun, 1200-1700. Admission free.* ⚏ 🅿 ♿ 🔥 🐕 ⚏

✤ **NEATISHEAD** *(nr. Norwich)* G4
WILLOW FARM FLOWERS, CANGATE,
NEATISHEAD, NR. NORWICH NR12 8YH
TEL: 01603 783588 FAX: 01603 783588
Located east of Wroxham off the A1151 - follow the brown signs.

One of the largest displays of dried, silk and parchment flowers in the region. Showfield. *Open: All year, Tues-Sat, 1000-1600; Sun, 1400-1600. Closed Mon (except Bank Hols, 1000-1600). Closed during Jan. Admission free.* 🏠 ⚏ 🅿 🎋 ♿

✤ **NORWICH** F5
THE PLANTATION GARDEN,
4 EARLHAM ROAD, NORWICH
TEL: 01603 611669
On Earlham Road (B1180), between the Beeches and Crofters Hotels (close to R.C. Cathedral).

Unusual surviving example of high Victorian garden, undergoing restoration. Varied levels and perspectives from paths, terraces and rustic bridge. **Features:** Garden folly (gothic fountain, rockworks, rustic bridge).

Parterre and sunken gardens. *Open: Mid Apr to Oct, Sun, 1400-1700. £1/£1/free (if accompanied by an adult).* ⚏ ⚏ ♿ 🔥 🐕 ♿

✤ **OXBOROUGH** *(nr. King's Lynn)* C5
◉ OXBURGH HALL, GARDENS AND ESTATE (The National Trust),
OXBOROUGH,
NR. KING'S LYNN PE33 9PS
TEL: 01366 328258 FAX: 01366 328066
At Oxborough, seven miles southwest of Swaffham.

A moated manor house built in 1482 by the Bedingfeld family who still live there. Colourful gardens with French parterre and woodland walks. Inside there are rare needlework hangings by Mary Queen of Scots. **Features:** Herbaceous borders. Fruit and vegetable, kitchen, parterre and wildflower gardens. *Open: House - 1-26 Apr + 1-29 Oct, Sat, Sun, Tue, Wed and Bank Hol Mon. 29 Apr-31 Jul + 1-30 Sept daily (not Thurs & Fri) Aug daily. Times: 1300-1700. Bank Hol Mon 1100-1700. Open: Gardens - 4-26 Mar, Sat & Sun. 1 Apr-31 Jul + 1 Sept - 29 Oct daily except Thurs & Fri. Aug daily. Times: 4-26 Mar 1100-1600. 1 April-29 Oct 1100-1730. House & garden £5.30/£5.30/£2, garden only £2.60/£2.60/£1.25.* ⬚ 🅿 ♿ ✕ ♿ ♿
SE - please telephone for details

✤ **RAVENINGHAM** *(nr. Norwich)* G6
RAVENINGHAM HALL GARDENS,
RAVENINGHAM,
NR. NORWICH NR14 6NS
TEL: 01508 548222 FAX: 01508 548958
Follow the brown signs from the A146 (Norwich to Lowestoft road) at Hales.

Extensive gardens surrounding an elegant Georgian house with many rare, variegated and unusual plants and shrubs, with sculptures, parkland and church. **Features:** Arboretum, herbaceous borders, landscaped parkland and statuary/sculpture. Herb, kitchen and Rose gardens. *Open: Apr, May, Jun and Jul, Sun, 1400-1700. Easter Sun and Mon, 1400-1700. £2/£2/free.* ⚏ 🅿 ♿ ✕ ♿ 🐕

❋ **REYMERSTON** *(nr. Norwich)* *E5*
❀ THORNCROFT CLEMATIS NURSERY,
THE LINGS, REYMERSTON,
NR. NORWICH NR9 4QG
TEL: 01953 850407 FAX: 01953 851788
On B1135, exactly halfway between Wymondham and Dereham.

A specialist Clematis nursery with beautiful display garden, dedicated to Clematis. Shrub and herbaceous borders, and vast collection of 'classic' Roses. **Features:** Sunken garden. *Open: 1 Mar to 31 Oct, daily (except Wed), 1000-1630. Admission free.* ♣ P wc ✗ ⅄

❋ **ROUGHTON** *(nr. Cromer)* *F3*
❀ FELBRIGG HALL, GARDENS AND PARK (The National Trust),
ROUGHTON, NORWICH NR11 8PR
TEL: 01263 837444 FAX: 01263 837032
Two miles south-west of Cromer on the B1436 (signposted off the A140 and A148).

The gardens at Felbrigg include a fully restored 18th century walled garden with dovecote and a typically Victorian 'American' garden to the north of the hall. There is also a seventeenth century Orangery which now contains some splendid Camellias planted in the nineteenth century. **Features:** Fruit and vegetable garden. National Collection of Colchicum. *Open: 1 Apr to 30 Oct, daily except Thurs and Fri, 1300-1700. Bank hol Sun and Mon 1100-1700. Garden as house 1100-1730. House - £5.70/£5.70/£2.80 Garden only £2.20/ £2.20/£1.* ⅏ ♣ P wc ✗ ⅄ ➤ ✗ & SE - please telephone for details.

❋ **SANDRINGHAM** *B/C3/4*
❀ SANDRINGHAM, THE ESTATE OFFICE, SANDRINGHAM PE35 6EN
TEL: 01553 772675 FAX: 01485 541571
From the A148, eight miles north-east of King's Lynn - follow the brown signs.

Sixty acres of glorious gardens surrounding the country retreat of H.M. The Queen, form a delightful spectacle throughout the seasons. Lawns and lakes, dells and glades, shrubs and trees create colour and contrast with interest, both historical and horticultural. Sandringham House and Museum are also open to the public. Guided garden tours available. **Features:** Arboretum and landscaped parkland. Dell, water and woodland gardens. **G** - William Broderick Thomas and Sir Geoffrey Jellicoe. *Open: Easter to mid Jul, and early Aug to Oct (plus weekends in Oct), daily, 1030-1700. Closed Good Friday. Please telephone for admission prices.* ⅏ ♣ P wc ➤ ✗ ⅄ & SE - 26 Jul.

❋ **SAXTHORPE** *(nr. Norwich)* *E3*
❀ MANNINGTON GARDENS,
MANNINGTON HALL, SAXTHORPE,
NR. NORWICH NR11 7BB
TEL: 01263 584175 FAX: 01263 761214
Signposted from B1149, Norwich to Holt road.

Beautiful gardens surrounding a medieval moated hall, with outstanding Rose gardens, lake, trees, shrubs and borders, as well as an extensive footpath network. Over 1,500 varieties of Roses feature in trees, in well-established borders and in the Heritage Rose Garden (in date order within period settings). **Features:** Arboretum, garden folly (temple), herbaceous borders, landscaped parkland and statuary/sculpture. Fruit and vegetable, kitchen, scent, Rose and wildflower gardens. *Open: May to Sept, Sun, 1200-1700.*

cont. next page

Jun to Aug, Wed, Thurs and Fri, 1100-1700. £3/ £2.50/free (if accompanied by an adult). ♿ ❀ P wc ▪ ☐ ✕ ✗ ⚲ SE - please telephone for details.

❀ **SISLAND** *(nr. Loddon)*   *G5/6*
JENNY BURGESS ALPINES,
1 RECTORY COTTAGE, SISLAND,
NR. LODDON NR14 6EF
TEL: 01508 520724
Take Sisland turning from A146, and follow signs to Sisland.

Cottage garden, with adjoining alpine and grasses nursery. **Features:** Herbaceous borders, fruit, vegetable, herb, kitchen and rock/alpine gardens. National Collection of Sisyrinchium. *Open: At most times, but advisable to telephone in advance to confirm visit. Admission free.* ❀ P wc SE - 11 Jun.

❀ **SOUTH WALSHAM**   *G4/5*
❂ FAIRHAVEN WOODLAND AND
WATER GARDEN, SCHOOL ROAD,
SOUTH WALSHAM NR13 6DZ
Nine miles north-east of Norwich on the B1140. Follow brown and white signs.

cont. next column

The largest collection of naturalised Candelabra Primulas in England. A host of rare and unusual shrubs and plants, children's nature trail, boat trips and wildlife sanctuary make Fairhaven a day out to remember. **Features:** Water, wildflower and woodland gardens. Special collection of Candelabra Primulas. *Open: daily, 1000-1700 (closed Christmas day). Open Wed and Thurs evening until 2100 in May, Jun, July & Aug. £3/£2.70/£1.00/under five's free.* ♿ ❀ P wc ☐ ✕ ✗ ☇ ⚲ SE - 16-30 Apr, 14-31 May, 22 Oct-30 Nov.

❀ **TERRINGTON ST. CLEMENT**
(nr. King's Lynn)

❂ AFRICAN VIOLET CENTRE,   *A4*
STATION ROAD, TERRINGTON
ST. CLEMENT, KING'S LYNN PE34 4PL
TEL: 01553 828374 FAX: 01553 827520
Beside A17 at Terrington St. Clement, three miles from A17/A47 junction.

Working nursery specialising in African Violets. Spectacular displays of many different colours and varieties. A selection of seasonal garden and houseplants is also available. *Open: All year, daily, 1000-1700 (or dusk if earlier). Admission free.* ♿ ❀ P wc ▪ ✕ ✗ ⚲

ORNAMENTAL CONIFERS AND   *A4*
HEATHERS, 22 CHAPEL ROAD,
TERRINGTON ST. CLEMENT,
NR. KING'S LYNN PE34 4ND
TEL: 01553 828874
Five miles from King's Lynn, off the A17.

Conifer and Heather display gardens. Japanese garden with Bonsai. **Features:** Japanese garden. *Open: 1 Feb to 20 Dec, daily, 0930-1700. Admission free.* ❀ P

North Norfolk Coast – Poppyland

Poppyland is the lovely name given to the area of North Norfolk, which stretches to the east and west of the village of Overstrand. It was here from August 1883, that the travel writer, Clement Scott, produced a series of articles, published in the Daily Telegraph, which brought the area fame and prosperity. In his articles he described how his walks along the cliffs took him through fields ablaze with Poppies at harvest time. Soon, the rich and famous were attracted to live at Overstrand and hundreds of holidaymakers travelled on the Great Eastern Railway's 'Poppy Line' to Cromer. New hotels were developed and 'Poppyland' souvenirs produced. But after Scott's death in 1904, like all crazes, the Poppyland mania began to fade, and by 1912 it had virtually disappeared.

THETFORD — *D6/7*

THE ANCIENT HOUSE MUSEUM,
WHITE HART STREET,
THETFORD IP24 1AA
TEL: 01842 752599

Follow signs for the town centre, museum is just up from The Bell Hotel.

Small Tudor-style herb garden designed to complement the 1490 Grade I listed house. **Features:** Herb garden. *Open: All year, Mon-Sat, 1000-1230 and 1300-1700. Jun to Aug, Sun, 1400-1700. Admission free (except in Jul and Aug - 70p/50p/40p). (nearby)*

KING'S HOUSE GARDEN, — *D6/7*
behind KING'S HOUSE,
THETFORD IP24 2AP
TEL: 01842 754247 FAX: 01842 762567

Follow signs to the town centre, King's House is opposite The Bell Hotel.

A mixed garden of mature trees, shrubs, Roses, lawns, herbaceous and formal borders. **Features:** Herbaceous borders. Rose garden. Special collection of Hardy Geraniums. *Open: All year, daily, 0730 to dusk (1930 Summer). Admission free.*

UPPER SHERINGHAM — *E/F2/3*

SHERINGHAM PARK
(The National Trust),
UPPER SHERINGHAM,
NR. SHERINGHAM NR26 8TB
TEL: 01263 823778 FAX: 01263 823778

Two miles south-west of Sheringham off the A148 (Cromer to Holt road).

Designed by Humphry Repton in 1812, this landscaped park contains mature woodland, and is famous for its Rhododendrons and Azaleas (flowering mid May-Jun). Spectacular views of the coast with viewing towers. Woodland, park and coastal walks. Features: Garden folly temple and landscaped parkland. G - Humphry Repton. *Open: All year, daily, dawn to dusk. £2.60 (per car).*

WALSINGHAM — *D3*

WALSINGHAM ABBEY GROUNDS
AND SHIREHALL MUSEUM,
WALSINGHAM NR22 6BP
TEL: 01328 820259 FAX: 01328 820098

From Fakenham B1105 (4 miles), from Norwich A1067 (27 miles).

A place of pilgrimage for 700 years, the ruins of Walsingham Abbey are set in landscaped parkland and grounds, through which the River Stiffkey runs. Massed displays of snowdrops. *Open: Please telephone for details of opening times. (nearby)* SE - Jan/Feb snowdrop walks

Flowers of the Field

Throughout the year, a drive through the rich farming countryside of the East of England reveals blankets of colourful flowers, some grown for commercial reasons, others of the wild variety. At Springtime, the dark days of winter are pushed aside by the unmistakable bright yellow of the Oilseed Rape. Later, as the summer months bring warmth and stability, Sweet William, Statice, Gladioli and many other beauties come into bloom. These are mainly picked by hand and sent off to market to cheer-up town and city dwellers. While in the fields, the rich blue of Flax (or Linseed Oil), the yellow of Mustard Seed and the lilac blues and mauves of Lavender provide a patchwork of colours across the landscape. Probably the most famous 'flower of the fields' is the Poppy whose lovely bright red heads seem to appear, scattered with wild abandon, throughout the countryside.

BRESSINGHAM
A Gardener's Paradise

✽ Two world renowned 6 acre gardens in delightful settings, over 8,000 species and varieties of plants and a chance to obtain many of them at Bressingham Plant Centre.

✽ Alan Bloom's Dell Garden – over 5,000 species and varieties of hardy perennials is open from April 1st 2000 until October 31st every day. Bressingham Steam Museum is nearby and is an attraction for all the family. Both from 1030-1700.

✽ Adrian Bloom's garden at Foggy Bottom nearby is completely separate, 6 acres of year round interest with wonderful vistas and plant associations. Separate entry charges. April 2nd to 31st October, every afternoon except Saturday and Monday from 1230-1630 and Bank Holidays.

✽ Special open "Gardeners Weekends"; 4-5 March, "Winter into Spring", 2-3 September, "Summer into Autumn", 1030-1700.

Bressingham lies 2½ miles west of Diss, Norfolk on the A1066.
For more details phone 01379 687402

56

Fairhaven Garden Trust, Norfolk

✤ **BOXFORD** *(nr. Sudbury)* *D9/10*
◎ THE HERALDIC GARDEN AND LADY HILDA MEMORIAL ARBORETUM, BOXFORD HOUSE, BOXFORD, NR. SUDBURY CO10 5JT
TEL: 01787 210208 FAX: 01787 211626
On the corner of the A1071 and Stone Street road (entrance off latter).

Founded in 1983, the Heraldic Garden is understood to be the only one of its kind in the world, combining a selection of fauna and flora found in heraldry, and forming the examples used in audio-peripatetic (hearing and strolling) presentations. **Features:** Arboretum, herbaceous borders and landscaped parkland. Herb, Rose and water gardens. *Open: 1 Jun to 30 Aug, Mon-Fri (pre-booked tours only), 0900-dusk. Individuals and small parties (less than 10), by prior arrangement. £8/£5.50/£3.* 🅿 wc 🎋 🎋 🎋 🎋 ⅏

BRANDON *C6*
◎ BRANDON COUNTRY PARK WALLED GARDEN, BURY ROAD, BRANDON IP27 0SU
TEL: 01842 810185 FAX: 01842 810185
Just south of Brandon on the B1106.

Originally built to supply Brandon Park House, the flint walled garden has been transformed to include both familiar old favourites, and some more unusual plants. **Features:** Herbaceous borders. Scent and herb garden. *Open: All year, Mon-Fri, 0900-1700; Sat and Sun, 0900-1730. Admission free.* ⅏ 🅿 wc 🎋 🎋 🎋 ⅏

✤ **BRUISYARD** *(nr. Saxmundham)* *G8*
◎ BRUISYARD VINEYARD AND HERB CENTRE, CHURCH ROAD, BRUISYARD, NR. SAXMUNDHAM IP17 2EF
TEL: 01728 638281 FAX: 01728 638442
Follow brown signs from A12 at Saxmundham.

Ten acre vineyard and winery. Tranquil water and herb gardens, with extensive range of herbs for sale. **Features:** Vineyard. Herb and water gardens. *Open: All year, daily, 1030-1700. Closed Christmas to New Year period. Admission free to gardens. Vineyard tour - £3.50/£3/£2.* ⅏ 🎋 🅿 wc ⅏ 🎋 ✗ 🎋 *(in vineyard only)* ⅏

✤ **BURY ST. EDMUNDS**

◎ THE ABBEY GARDENS, *C/D8*
BURY ST. EDMUNDS IP33 1XL
TEL: 01284 757490 FAX: 01284 757091
From A14, take central exit to Historic Bury St. Edmunds, and follow signs to 'historic town centre'.

Prize winning public gardens centred around the ruins of the Abbey of St. Edmund, including a host of ducks and squirrels, a children's play area and games. Winner of Britain in Bloom 1999. Beautiful bedding displays all year round set the tone for the annual Bury in Bloom campaign. The aviary and ice-cream kiosk are popular with all the family. **Features:** Pilgrims' Herb Garden, annual bedding, herbaceous borders and public park. Rock/alpine, rose and water gardens. 🅶 - Nathaniel Hodson. *Open: All year, Mon-Sat from 0730; Sun from 0900. Closes half an hour before dusk. Admission free.* ⅏ 🎋 *(at certain times of the year)* 🅿 *(five mins walk away)* wc ⅏ 🎋 🎋 🎋 ⅏ SE -12, 26-28 May, many others arranged, please telephone for details

◎ HARDWICK HEATH, *C/D8*
HARDWICK LANE, BURY ST. EDMUNDS, SUFFOLK
TEL: 01284 763666
On the outskirts of the town, situated off Hardwick Lane.

Fifty-five acres of parkland with superb 200 year old Cedar of Lebanon trees. Tree gallery trail available. **Features:** Arboretum and landscaped parkland and wildflower garden. *Open: All year, daily, dawn to dusk. Admission free.* 🅿 wc 🎋 🎋 🎋 SE - all year round, contact TIC for details

☉ NOWTON PARK, *C/D8*
NOWTON ROAD,
BURY ST. EDMUNDS
TEL: 01284 763666

Leave A14 at 'east' exit, and follow tourist signs (for one mile).

Two hundred acre Victorian-style country estate, famous for its avenue of Daffodils in the Spring. Magnificent specimen trees, ponds and over two hundred species of wildflower. **Features:** Arboretum, folly, landscaped parkland, and maze. Wildflower garden. *Open: All year, daily, 0830 to dusk. Admission free.* ♿ 🅿 🚾 🛉 🏕 🐕 ♿ SE - 18 Jun

☉ PILGRIMS' HERB GARDEN, *C/D8*
ST. EDMUNDSBURY CATHEDRAL,
ANGEL HILL,
BURY ST. EDMUNDS IP33 1LS
TEL: 01284 754933 FAX: 01284 768655

Entrance through cathedral cloisters, or on right through Abbey Gate (from Angel Hill).

A new fragrant and stimulating garden, the inspiration of author/herb gardener Leslie Bremness. Many of the herbs are based on the Bury Herbal, written by the monks of the once great abbey. **Features:** Herbaceous borders and statuary/sculpture. Herb garden. *Open: All year, Mon-Sat from 0730; Sun from 0900. Closes half an hour before dusk. Admission free.* ♿ 🅿 *(five mins walk away)* 🚾 🛒 ✕ 🛉 🐕 ♿

❋ CHARSFIELD *(nr. Woodbridge)* *F8*
SISKIN PLANTS,
DAVEY LANE, CHARSFIELD,
NR. WOODBRIDGE IP13 7QG
TEL: 01473 737567 FAX: 01473 737567

North of Woodbridge (A12), first left 'Bredfield' to B1078 - turn right. First left in Charsfield.

Specialist nursery growing wide range of alpines and dwarf plants. Friendly advice always available. **Features:** Rock/alpine garden. National Collection of Hebe (dwarf - East Anglia). *Open: Mar to Oct, Tues-Sat, 1000-1700. Admission free.* 🌿 🅿 🐕

Bury St. Edmunds

If you love flowers, then you'll love Bury St. Edmunds in Suffolk. From June to September, this historic market town is filled with the perfumes and colours of summer flowers, with hanging baskets, window boxes and bedding displays turning the town into a giant, living garden. Its twelve years of floral excellence have seen it become the 'Floral Town of Britain' in 1988, and **now in 1999 the National Winner of the Britain in Bloom competition.**

❋ CODDENHAM *(nr. Ipswich)* *E/F9*
SHRUBLAND PARK GARDEN,
SHRUBLAND PARK,
CODDENHAM, NR. IPSWICH IP6 9QQ
TEL: 01473 830221 FAX: 01473 832202

From A140/A14 intersection, take slip road to A14 (Ipswich). On slip road turn left to Barham.

Extensive formal gardens - one of the finest examples of Italianate gardens in England. Evergreens clipped into architectural shapes, complement the hard landscaping of the masonry. Sir Charles Barry exploited the chalk escarpment overlooking the Gipping Valley to create the magnificent 'Grand Descent' which links the Hall to the lower gardens. **Features:** Garden folly (grand stairs), herbaceous borders, landscaped parkland, maze (box hedge) and statuary/sculpture. Dell, Italian, rock/alpine and wildflower gardens. 🄶 - William Robinson and Sir Charles Barry. *Open: 9 Apr to 24 Sept, Sun and Bank Hol Mon, 1400-1700. £2.50/£1.50/£1.50.* 🅿 🚾 🏕 🛉

❋ DUNWICH *(nr. Saxmundham)* *H7/8*
☉ DUNWICH HEATH (The National Trust), THE COASTGUARD COTTAGES,
DUNWICH HEATH,
NR. SAXMUNDHAM IP17 3DJ
TEL: 01728 648505 FAX: 01728 648384

Signposted from A12 at Yoxford and Blythburgh. Two miles south of Dunwich village.

cont. next page

One of Suffolk's most important conservation areas. Magnificent purple and pink heather and golden gorse. Field study centre and public hide. Many types of birds, butterfiles and insects. *Open: All year, daily, dawn to dusk. Small parking charge (£1.70)* ♿ & ✗ (daily except Mon, hours vary). 🅿 ♿ 🍴 ⚹ 🐕 ⚹ SE - please telephone for details

✤ EAST BERGHOLT *E10*
◉ EAST BERGHOLT PLACE GARDEN, EAST BERGHOLT CO7 6UP
TEL: 01206 299224 FAX: 01206 299224
Two miles east of the A12, on the B1070 (edge of East Bergholt village).

Fifteen acre garden and arboretum, laid out at the turn of the century by the present owners great grandfather. Renowned for its Camellias, Magnolias and Rhododendrons. Many rare and unusual trees, two ornamental ponds and fine topiary Yew hedges. A plant centre has been set up in the walled garden. **Features:** Arboretum and topiary. Wildflower bank. 🄶 - (plant collector) George Forrest. *Open: 1 Mar to 30 Sept, daily, 1000-1700. Closed Easter Sunday. £2/£2/free.* ⚹ 🅿 ♿ &

✤ EYKE *(nr. Woodbridge)* *G9*
THE ROOKERY GARDEN AND VINEYARD, THE ROOKERY, EYKE, NR. WOODBRIDGE IP12 2RR
TEL: 01394 460226 FAX: 01394 460818
Turn left off B1084, three miles east of Melton. Garden is half a mile on right.

Nine acre garden with shrubs, Roses, bulbs and borders. Set amongst grass paths on different levels, and amidst trees and Rhododendrons. **Features:** Vineyard. Japanese garden. *Open: 9, 30 Apr, 14 May, 4, 18, 25 Jun, 16 Jul, 17 Sept. Sun 1400-1730. £2.50/£2/50p.* ⚹ 🅿 ♿ 🍴 ✗ &

✤ FELIXSTOWE *G10*
◉ FELIXSTOWE - 'SEAFRONT GARDENS'
Off Sea Road and Undercliff Road East.

Felixstowe - "the Garden Resort of the East Coast". Seafront and cliff gardens, with special set pieces including a water clock, grotto and waterfall. **Features:** Arboretum, garden folly, rock grotto, herbaceous borders and landscaped parkland. Italian garden. *Open: All year, daily, any reasonable time. Admission free.* ♿ 🅿 ♿ 🐕 &

✤ FRAMLINGHAM *F/G8*
◉ SHAWSGATE VINEYARD, BADINGHAM ROAD, FRAMLINGHAM IP13 9HZ
TEL: 01728 724060 FAX: 01728 723232
Follow the brown tourist signs, from both the A12 and B1120.

Fifteen acre vineyard, making award winning English wines. Tours and vine leasing available. Shop selling a range of wines and wine related items. **Features:** Vineyard. *Open: 1 Feb to 24 Dec, daily, 1030-1700. £3.25/£2.75/free (under 14yrs).* ♿ ⚹ 🅿 ♿ 🍴 ⚹ 🐕

✤ HADLEIGH *E9*
GUILDHALL GARDEN, MARKET PLACE, HADLEIGH IP7 5DJ
TEL: 01473 827752
In the town centre, entrance at rear of Guildhall, on footpath between Market Place and churchyard.

Small enclosed town garden opened in 1997. Designed to complement medieval timber framed Guildhall with traditional plants and features. Cream teas served. **Features:** Maze (brick). Herb and knot gardens. 🄶 - Cedric Morris. *Open: 1430 - 1700 Jun to end of Sept, Sun to Fri (closed Sats). Admission free.* ♿ ✗ ⚹ 🐕

✤ **HARTEST** *(nr. Bury St. Edmunds)* C9
◉ GIFFORDS HALL VINEYARD AND
SWEET PEA CENTRE, HARTEST,
NR. BURY ST EDMUNDS IP29 4EX
TEL: 01284 830464
From A134, midway between Bury St Edmunds and Sudbury - follow the brown tourist signs.

Vineyard with wildflower meadows, Sweet Peas grown for exhibition, one acre Rose garden and organic vegetable garden. **Features:** Woodland, fruit and vegetable and Rose garden. *Open: Easter to Oct 31, daily, 1100-1800. £3.25/£2.75/free.* ♿ ♨ 🅿 ᵂᶜ 🍴 🜲 ✕ ✗ ↑ ⅊ SE - 24, 25 Jun, 2, 23, 24 Sept.

✤ **HAUGHLEY** *(nr. Stowmarket)* E8
HAUGHLEY PARK, HAUGHLEY,
NR. STOWMARKET IP14 3JY
TEL: 01359 240701 FAX: 01359 240546
Four miles west of Stowmarket, signposted off the A14 'Haughley Park' (not Haughley).

Imposing red-brick Jacobean manor house set in six acres of well tended gardens, including walled kitchen garden. Park and woodland, with three walks (1.5-2.5 miles). **Features:** Arboretum, herbaceous borders and landscaped parkland. Dell, fruit and vegetable, kitchen and woodland gardens. *Open: May to Sept, Tues, 1400-1730. Also Suns 30 Apr and 7 May (for Bluebell display). House open by appointment only. £2/£2/£1.* 🅿 ᵂᶜ 🜲 ↑ ⅊ SE - 30 Apr and 7 May.

✤ **HAVERHILL** B9
EAST TOWN PARK,
COUPALS ROAD,
HAVERHILL
TEL: 01440 710745 FAX: 01440 710745
Sturmer Road out of Haverhill, under viaduct, second left, then first right.

Country Park, 30 acres with children's play area. Centre open at weekends, refreshments and gifts. Walks. **Features:** Landscaped parkland. Wildflower garden. *Open: 0900 - dusk all year round. Admission free.* ♿ 🅿 ᵂᶜ 🜲 ✗ ↑ ⅊ SE - throughout the year contact TIC (01284) 764667 for details.

✤ **HELMINGHAM** *(nr. Stowmarket)* F8
◉ HELMINGHAM HALL GARDENS,
THE ESTATE OFFICE, HELMINGHAM,
NR. STOWMARKET IP14 6EF
TEL: 01473 890363 FAX: 01473 890776
On the B1077, nine miles north of Ipswich.

Grade I listed hall with two Rose gardens, including a 19th century parterre, an incomparable Elizabethan kitchen garden, and a herb garden based on historical themes. **Features:** Herbaceous borders, landscaped parkland and topiary. Fruit and vegetable, herb, kitchen, knot, parterre, rose and wildflower gardens. *Open: 30 Apr to 10 Sept, Sun, 1400-1800. Also Wed (during same period), by appointment only, 1400-1700. £3.75/£3.75/£2/ £3.25 (Groups)* ♿ ♨ 🅿 ᵂᶜ 🜲 ✕ ✗ *(on Wed)* ↑ ⅊

✤ **HORRINGER** *(nr. Bury St. Edmunds)* C8
◉ ICKWORTH HOUSE, PARK AND
GARDENS (The National Trust),
THE ROTUNDA, HORRINGER,
NR. BURY ST. EDMUNDS IP29 5QE
TEL: 01284 735270 FAX: 01284 735175
In the village of Horringer, three miles southwest of Bury St. Edmunds (on west side of A143).

Ickworth House is surrounded by an Italianate garden, and set in a 'Capability' Brown park with woodland walks, vineyard, Georgian summerhouse, canal and lake. **Features:** Arboretum, garden folly (temple and summer-houses), herbaceous borders, landscaped parkland and vineyard. Italian, scent, wildflower and woodland gardens. National Collection of Buxus (box). Special collection of Ligustrum (privet) and Phillyrea. **Ꮐ** - Lancelot 'Capability' Brown. *Open: House - 18 Mar - 29 Oct, daily (except Mon/Thur), 1300-1700. Open Bank Hol Mon. Closed 1630 in Oct. Garden - 18 Mar - 29 Oct, daily, 1000-1700; 1 Nov to March (2000), Mon-Fri, 1000-1600. Park - all year, daily (except 25 Dec), 0700-1900. House, park and gardens - £5.50/£5.50/£2.40. Park & gardens only - £2.20/£2.20/70p. Family discounts available.* ♿ ♨ 🅿 ᵂᶜ 🜲 ✕ ✗ ↑*(park only)* ⅊ SE - Apr, Wood Fair; Sept 17, Plant Fair, please telephone for details.

SUFFOLK

‡ **LAVENHAM** *(nr. Sudbury)*

◎ THE GUILDHALL   *D9*
OF CORPUS CHRISTI (The National Trust),
MARKET PLACE,
LAVENHAM CO10 9QZ
TEL: 01787 247646
*In Lavenham from the Swan Hotel, turn left into
Lady Street (which leads into the Market Place).*

An early 16th century timber-framed
building with a restored 19th century
lock-up and mortuary. Walled garden with
dye plants used in woollen cloth trade.
Features: Walled courtyard garden with
specimen dye plants as used medieval trade.
*Open: Mar - Nov, Sat and Sun only 1100-1600.
1-20 Apr, Thurs - Sun 1100-1700, (closed Good
Fri), 22 Apr - 5 Nov, daily, 1100-1700. £3/£3/children
free (if accompanied by an adult).* ♿ 🅿 (adjacent,
not NT) 🚾 ♨ ✕ 🎃

◎ LITTLE HALL, MARKET PLACE,   *D9*
LAVENHAM, NR. SUDBURY CO10 9QZ
TEL: 01787 247543 FAX: 01787 248341
A delightful English country garden, which
is part of the history of Lavenham, being
the garden of a 14th century hall house,
which was a home for nearly 600 years.
Features: Herbaceous borders. Herb and
rose garden. *Open: Apr to end Oct, Wed, Thurs,
Sat and Sun, 1400-1730; Bank Hols, 1100-1730.
Admission £1.50/£1.50/children free (if accompanied
by an adult), unaccompanied 50p.* 🎃

‡ **LITTLE BLAKENHAM** *(nr. Ipswich)* E9
BLAKENHAM WOODLAND GARDEN,
LITTLE BLAKENHAM,
NR. IPSWICH IP8 4LZ
TEL: 01473 833249
Four miles north-west of Ipswich, off the B1113.

Five acre woodland garden, with many rare
trees and shrubs, Camellias, Magnolias,
Azaleas, Rhododendrons, Roses and Bluebells.
Especially lovely in the Spring. **Features:**
Woodland garden. *Open: 1 Mar to 30 Jun, daily
(except Sat), 1300-1700, £1/£1/£1.* 🅿

‡ **LONG MELFORD** *(nr. Sudbury)*   D9

◎ KENTWELL HALL, LONG MELFORD,
NR. SUDBURY CO10 9BA
TEL: 01787 310207 FAX: 01787 379318
*Signposted off the A143, ten miles south of Bury
St. Edmunds.*

A beautiful moated red-brick Tudor manor,
Kentwell has extensive gardens restored to
their 16th century design, as well as
woodland walks. **Features:** Landscaped
parkland. Fruit and vegetable, herb,
sunken and wildflower gardens. *Open: Mar
to Oct (not daily). Please telephone for opening
times and admission prices.* ♿ 🅿 🚾 ♨ 🍴 ✕ 🎃

◎ MELFORD HALL   *D9*
(The National Trust), LONG MELFORD,
NR. SUDBURY CO10 9AH
TEL: 01787 880286
*In Long Melford on east side of A134, fourteen
miles south of Bury St. Edmunds.*

One of East Anglia's most celebrated
Elizabethan houses. A small garden has
some spectacular specimen trees and a
charming Summer house. There is a walk
through the park. **Features:** Garden
folly (Tudor pavilion), herbaceous borders,
landscaped parkland and topiary. *Open: Apr
and Oct, Sat, Sun and Bank Hol Mon, 1400-
1730. May to Sept, Wed-Sun and Bank Hol Mon,
1400-1730. £4.30/£4.30/£2.* 🅿 🚾

SUN HOUSE, HALL STREET,   *D9*
LONG MELFORD CO10 9HZ
TEL: 01787 378252
In the main street, opposite The Cock and Bell pub.

Award-winning garden, featured on television
and in magazines. Double walled gardens,
with 100 varieties of Clematis, Roses, rare
herbaceous plants, fountains, pools, trees,
shrubs and shell folly. **Features:** Garden
folly, herbaceous borders and statuary/sculpture.
Italian, Rose and scent gardens. *Open: 23 Apr,
1 May, 4, 11, 17, 18, 25 Jun, 2, 9 Jul, 1400-1800.
£2.50/£2.50/free (under 16yrs).* 🏕 🅿 🎃 ♿

62

✤ **MICKFIELD** *E/F8*
MICKFIELD WATERGARDEN CENTRE,
DEBENHAM ROAD, MICKFIELD,
NR. STOWMARKET IP14 5LP
TEL: 01449 711336 FAX: 01449 711018
*From A140 - go into Mickfield village, go straight
over crossroads, follow the tourist signs.*

Two acres of ornamental water gardens to
enjoy. Nursery specialists in established
water and pond-side plants. **Features:**
Herbaceous borders. Water gardens.
Open: All year, daily, 0930-1700. Admission free.
✿ 🅿 ⁅ᵂᶜ⁆ ♿ ✕ 🐾 ⅃

✤ **MONKS ELEIGH** *(nr. Ipswich)* *D9*
◉ CORN CRAFT, MONKS ELEIGH,
NR. IPSWICH IP7 7AY
TEL: 01449 740456 FAX: 01449 741665
On the A1141 between Hadleigh and Lavenham.

Craft shop, tea room and flower shop
specialising in dried, silk and parchment-
flowers, including a full range of corn
dollies. Set in a delightful position, the
converted farm buildings overlook a paddock.
Tea room serves home made products, and
the gift shop specialises in local crafts.
*Open: All year, Mon-Sat, 1000-1700; Sun, 1100-
1700. Admission free.* ⏧ 🅿 ⁅ᵂᶜ⁆ ♿ ✕ 🐾 ⅃

✤ **SHIMPLING** *(nr. Bury St. Edmunds)* *D9*
LANDMARK GARDENS,
GATEFIELDS MEADOW, SHIMPLING,
NR. BURY ST. EDMUNDS IP29 4EX
TEL: 01284 830171/830181
FAX: 01284 830171
*Follow signs from A134 to Shimpling at Bridge
Street. A1066 - follow signs to Shimpling.*

Hilltop landscape garden on heavy clay.
Two and half acres began in 1993/94,
showing formal and informal landscaping
and plant associations, for an exposed site
on heavy alkaline clay. **Features:**
Arboretum, herbaceous borders and maze
(hedge). Mediterranean, parterre, Rose,
scent, water, wildflower and woodland

gardens. *Open: All year, daily, Summer (BST)
1100-1700; Winter (GMT) 1100-1600. Closed
Sat, Sept-Feb inclusive. £2/£2/£1 (includes free
tea or coffee).* ✿ 🅿 ✕ 🐾 ⅃ ♿

✤ **SOMERLEYTON** *(nr. Lowestoft)* *H6*
◉ SOMERLEYTON HALL & GARDENS,
SOMERLEYTON,
NR. LOWESTOFT NR32 5QQ
TEL: 01502 730224 FAX: 01502 732143
Internet: www.somerleyton.co.uk
*On B1074, five miles from Lowestoft, off A143
eight miles south of Great Yarmouth.*

Beautiful twelve acre gardens, surrounding
an early Victorian stately mansion. Magnificent
specimen trees, plants, borders and famous
English yew hedge maze. Victorian glass-
houses and original garden ornamentation.
The wide variety of plants grown, give
colour and interest throughout the year,
whilst specific features will delight both the
enthusiast and casual visitor alike. Walled
garden, glass houses, pergola, specimen trees.
Features: Herbaceous borders, maze
(hedge), statuary/sculpture and topiary.
Fruit and vegetable, kitchen, rose and
sunken gardens. 🅶 - William Nesfield and
Sir Joseph Paxton. *Open: Easter Sun to end
Sept, Thurs, Sun, Bank Hols (plus Tues and Wed
in Jul and Aug), 1230-1730. £5/£4.80/£2.50
family £14.20.* ⏧ ✿ 🅿 ⁅ᵂᶜ⁆ ♿ 🍴 ✕ ♿. *Pre-booked
guided tours available for groups.*

✤ **STANTON** *(nr. Bury St. Edmunds)* D7
**WYKEN HALL GARDENS AND WYKEN VINEYARDS, STANTON,
NR. BURY ST. EDMUNDS IP31 2DW**
TEL: 01359 250287 FAX: 01359 252256
From A143 at Ixworth, follow brown signs to Wyken Vineyards.

A garden of many rooms - Rose, herb, knot, red hot border, maze, wild and woodland plants. Much developed recently with fine trees and shrubs. **Features:** Garden folly (gazebo), herbaceous borders, maze (copper beech) and vineyard. Dell, fruit and vegetable, herb, kitchen, knot, parterre, Rose, scent, wildflower and woodland gardens. *Open: 1 Apr to 1 Oct, Bank Hol Mons, Wed, Thurs, Fri and Sun, 1000-1700. £2.50/£2/free (disabled visitors free).* ⚙ ♿ 🅿 🚾 ✕ 🐕 ♿

✤ **STOKE-BY-CLARE** *(nr. Sudbury)* C9
**BOYTON VINEYARD,
STOKE-BY-CLARE,
NR. SUDBURY CO10 8TB**
TEL: 01440 761893 FAX: 01440 761893
Signposted from the A1092.

A vineyard, with vines growing in the gardens of a listed period farmhouse. Tours are available with wine tastings. **Features:** Arboretum, herbaceous borders, landscaped parkland and vineyard. Dell, water and wildflower gardens. *Open: 1 Apr to 31 Oct, daily, 1100-1800. Admission free.* ⚙ 🅿 🚾 🎋 🐕 ♿

✤ **SUDBURY** D9
◉ **GAINSBOROUGH'S HOUSE,
46 GAINSBOROUGH STREET,
SUDBURY CO10 2EU**
TEL: 01787 372958 FAX: 01787 376991
Located in Sudbury town centre.

Birthplace of Thomas Gainsborough R.A. Georgian fronted town house with an attractive walled garden, containing 300 year old Mulberry tree. **Features:** Herb garden. *Open: All year, Tues-Sat, 1000-1700; Sun and Bank Hol Mon, 1400-1700. Closes at 1600 from Nov to Mar. Closed on Mon, Good Fri and Christmas period. £3/£2.50/£1.50.* ⚙ 🚾 🎋

✤ **WENHASTON** *(nr. Halesworth)* G/H7
**WOOTTENS PLANTS
BLACKHEATH, WENHASTON,
NR. HALESWORTH IP19 9HD**
TEL: 01502 478258
Signposted 600 yards south of Blythburgh, on the A12.

Woottens is famous for its huge range of herbaceous plants and Pelargonium's. The nursery and garden have been featured in 'Gardens Illustrated' and the 'RHS Journal'. "The plants are thumping with health, and the range is extraordinary. To get there I spent seven hours in the car driving through a monumental cloud burst, but it was worth it" - Anna Pavord, The Independent. **Features:** Garden folly and herbaceous borders. Special collection of Pelargonium's. *Open: Nursery - all year, daily, 0930-1700. Garden - 1 May to 30 Sept, Wed, 0930-1500. £1.50/50p/20p.* ♿ 🅿 🚾 ♿

✤ **WESTON** *(nr. Beccles)* G/H6
**HOME & GARDEN AT WINTER FLORA,
HALL FARM, WESTON,
NR. BECCLES NR34 8TT**
TEL: 01502 716810 FAX: 01502 717139
One and a half miles south of Beccles, on the A145.

A garden for the enjoyment of visitors to Winter Flora. Living willow hedge and arbour. The formal paths are lined with pale yellow santolina and deep purple lavender Hidcote. A profusion of unusual perennials and annuals fill the beds within the paths. After just three summers rambling roses

continued on next page

SUFFOLK

are smothering the central gazebo. Special features - In the herb garden a glorious mixture of hummocks and carpeting thymes. **Features:** Herbaceous borders and living Willow hedge and arbour. Herb, Rose & parterre gardens. *Open: All year, Mon-Sat, 1000-1700; Sun 1100-1700. Closed 24-29 Dec and Easter day. Admission free.* ⬛ ♣ 🅿 🆆🅲 ⬛
🏛 ✕ ⅄ ♿

✳ **WINGFIELD** *(nr. Stradbroke)*   *F7*
◉ WINGFIELD OLD COLLEGE AND GARDENS, WINGFIELD, NR. STRADBROKE IP21 5RA
TEL: 01379 384888 FAX: 01379 388082
From the A140 (Ipswich to Norwich road), follow the B1118 (and brown tourist signs). Also signposted off the B1116 at Fressingfield.

Four acre gardens, including eccentric topiary garden, old Roses, ancient ponds and 17th century walled garden. Unique to this garden is the collection of contemporary sculpture by artists including Michael Lyons, Martyn Welch and Lee Grandjean. Also topiary as sculpture. **Features:** Contemporary sculpture and topiary. Walled garden restoration project (Summer 2000). 🄶 - Ian Chance. *Open: From Easter Sat to end of Sept, Sat and Sun, 1400-1800. £3.80/£3/£2 (including Historic House and new arts centre)* 🅿 🆆🅲 ⬛ ✕ 𝒦 ♿

✳ **WOODBRIDGE**   *F/G9*
ELMHURST PARK, WOODBRIDGE
TEL: 01394 383599 FAX: 01394 384251

Adjacent to Lime Kiln Quay road and Quayside.
A delightful park with (all year round) colourful bedding displays. Children's play area, Summer concerts and brick-built maze. **Features:** Herbaceous borders, landscaped parkland and maze (brick). Dell garden. *Open: All year, daily, any reasonable time. Admission free.* 🅿 *(adjacent)* 🆆🅲 🏛 ⅄ ♿

65

Garden
DISCOVERY TOURS

Some of the gardens featured within these tours, have limited or restricted opening hours. We have indicated these with an *, and suggest you refer to their entry within this guide (to check opening times), before starting your journey.

GARDENS OF THE BROADS

Reed-fringed waterways, wildflowers, Primulas and Bananas! – discover the lovely woodland and tropical gardens of Britain's newest national park, the Norfolk Broads.

Starting point: Norwich (Norfolk) **Mileage:** 25 miles *Morning* – leave Norwich on the B1140 to South Walsham (about nine miles), to see the collection of Candelabra Primula at the Fairhaven Woodlands & Water Gardens. Then follow the unclassified road through the villages of Ranworth and Woodbastwick to Wroxham. *Afternoon* – leave the town by travelling north along the A1151, to visit the woodland gardens of Hoveton Hall. After your visit, remain on the A1151/A149 to Stalham. From the town centre, follow the unclassified road (north-west) to the village of East Ruston, where you can see Bananas growing at the exotic *East Ruston Old Vicarage.

BY ROYAL APPOINTMENT

From the exotic flowers of Africa, this tour will take you to the gardens of the Queen, and the sweet-smelling home of English Lavender.

Starting point: King's Lynn (Norfolk) **Mileage:** 23 miles *Morning* – leave King's Lynn on the A17 to Terrington St. Clement, and visit the colourful African Violet Centre. Then retrace your steps back to King's Lynn, and take the A149 north. After about six miles, turn right to join the B1439 to Sandringham. *Afternoon* – enjoy Sandringham's sixty acres of grounds, and the Queen's favourite blooms. When you are ready to leave, take the B1440 to the village of Dersingham. At the T-junction, turn right and follow the road to the round-about with the A149. Head north along the A149 to Heacham. End the day at the sweet-smelling home of Norfolk Lavender Limited.

BLOOMIN' BEAUTIFUL

Discover vines, Roses and Sweet Peas in some of the best gardens in Suffolk – we will even take you to Foggy Bottom! Choose from two options, both starting in the town of Bury St. Edmunds.

Starting point: Bury St. Edmunds *(Suffolk)* **Mileage:** *Option 1 – 21 miles, Option 2 – 12^1/$_2$miles*

Option 1

Morning – explore the award-winning gardens at Bury St. Edmunds, then leave the town on the A143 towards Diss. After seven miles, follow the signs to the secret gardens of Wyken Hall. *Afternoon* – retrace your steps to the A143, turn right and head to the village of Botesdale. Here you turn left onto the B1113 to South Lopham. At the T-junction, turn right onto the A1066 to visit Bressingham Gardens & Steam Museum, with its famous 'Foggy Bottom' & Dell gardens.

Option 2 *Morning* – explore the award-winning gardens at Bury St. Edmunds, then leave the town on the A143/B1066 south to the village of Hartest (about seven miles). Visit Gifford's Hall Vineyard & Sweet Pea Centre to see the prize-winning blooms. *Afternoon* – retrace your steps for five miles along the B1066, then turn left along an unclassified road to the village of Horringer. At the T-junction, turn right on the A143. Shortly on your left is the entrance to the unusual Ickworth House, Park & Gardens, with its Italian garden.

AUTUMN COLOURS

For a few weeks in October, the trees are ablaze with Autumn colours and shades. Enjoy them as you travel from Britain's largest lowland pine forest, to the orchards of Oxburgh Hall.

Starting point: Brandon *(Suffolk)* **Mileage:** 16 miles *Morning* – head south from the town along the B1106 (for about a half a mile) to visit the traditional blooms at the Brandon Country Park Walled Garden. Retrace your steps back to Brandon, this time heading north along the A1065 towards Swaffham. After five miles at the roundabout with the A134, follow the signs to Lynford

Arboretum. Enjoy a short stroll around the Conifers and broadleaves, then retrace your steps to the Mundford roundabout and take the A134 towards King's Lynn. After seven miles, at the roundabout in the village of Whittington, follow the brown signs to Oxburgh Hall, Garden & Estate. *Afternoon* – spend the rest of the day exploring the woodland and orchards of this moated hall.

COUNTRY CLASSICS

A classical tour of three grand country estates in the county of Norfolk, combining Repton's 'favourite landscape' at Sheringham, delightful Felbrigg, and the spectacular Blickling Hall.
Starting point: Cromer (Norfolk)
Mileage: 21$^{1/2}$ miles *Morning* – leave Cromer on the A148 towards Holt. After about five and a half miles, you will see the entrance to Sheringham Park. Start the day with a stroll through Humphry Repton's most favourite piece of landscape work. Then retrace your steps (for about four miles) along the A148 towards Cromer, and turn right onto the B1436 to Felbrigg Hall, Garden & Park. Explore the gardens of this 17th century house. *Afternoon* – Remain on the B1436 to Roughton. At the junction with the A140, turn right and follow this for seven miles to the town of Aylsham. Then take the B1354 to Blickling Hall, Park & Garden, with its massive yew hedges and herbaceous borders.

SUFFOLK'S SECRET GARDENS

Unlock the door on Suffolk's secret gardens, and discover a world of rare trees & strange topiary, an enchanting Bluebell wood, and the 'grand stairway' to Sir Charles Barry's masterpiece.
Starting point: East Bergholt (Suffolk)
Mileage: 17 miles *Morning* – explore the rare trees and topiary at East Bergholt Place Garden. *Afternoon* – leave the village on the B1070 to the A12, which you follow north towards Ipswich. At the junction with the A14, turn left to join this towards Bury St. Edmunds. After four and a half miles, leave the A14 to follow the B1113. Then about half a mile later, turn right along an unclassified road to Little Blakenham. Visit the secret

Blakenham Woodland Garden, with its Bluebell displays. Then retrace your steps to the A14, and rejoin this eastwards for three miles, to the next turn-off (the A140). Go around the roundabout, joining the slip road back onto the A14 westwards (back towards Ipswich). On this slip road, you turn left to Barham and *Shrubland Park Garden, designed by Sir Charles Barry.

NURSERY THYME

From aromatic herbs and Thymes to prize-winning Pelargoniums, dried flowers and a chance to get lost in a famous maze – discover the specialist gardens and nurseries of Suffolk.
Starting point: Framlingham (Suffolk)
Mileage: 37 miles *Morning* – leave the town on the B1120. After two miles, turn right along an unclassified road to Bruisyard Vineyard & Herb Centre. Enjoy a tasting of the wine, then retrace your steps to the B1120 and turn right. About half a mile later you reach the A1120, turn right and follow this to Yoxford. When you reach the junction with the A12, turn left towards Lowestoft. Then after five miles, turn left again, following the signs to Woottens Plants and its prize-winning Pelargoniums. *Afternoon* – Retrace your steps to the A12 and head to the village of Blythburgh. Here you turn left onto the A145 towards Beccles. After eight miles you reach the village of Weston, where a a short visit can be made to the dried flowers of Winter Flora. Then continue on the A145 (through Beccles) to the roundabout, where you turn left onto the A146. One mile later at the second roundabout, turn right onto the A143. After six miles, turn right again onto the B1074 to visit the Victorian Somerleyton Hall & Gardens, where you can get lost in the famous maze.

Norfolk Lavender, Norfolk

67

MAP OF NORFOLK & SUFFOLK

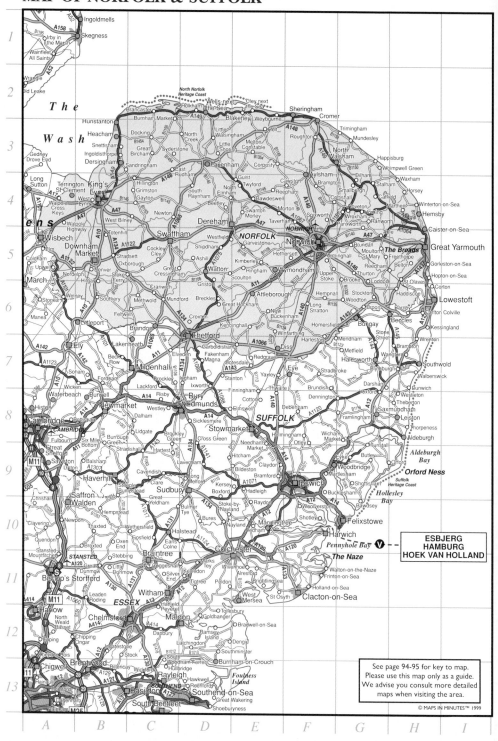

See page 94-95 for key to map.
Please use this map only as a guide.
We advise you consult more detailed
maps when visiting the area.

© MAPS IN MINUTES™ 1999

Hatfield House
Festival *of* Gardening

Saturday 24th & Sunday 25th June 2000

Hosted by Lady Salisbury and to be held for the eighteenth time on the South Front of the House, the Festival of Gardening is a landmark event in the gardens' calendar. The Flower Tent has displays by top national nurseries and growers and many gardening related trades attend. Together with all of the activities and events outlined below, a luncheon tent and barbeque and all of the spectacular organic formal gardens to enjoy, this is a marvellous day out for gardeners and their families. Coach parties are always very welcome.

10am	*FESTIVAL OPENS*

From 11am to 5pm:	• **FESTIVAL OF FLOWERS** *(in Hatfield House - additional charge £2)* • **NAFAS FLORAL DESIGN COMPETITION** *(Riding School)*

Throughout the day:	• **BIRDS OF PREY, HORSES, GUN DOGS & FERRETS** *(Showground)* • **THE JAMBALAYA JAZZ QUINTET** *(Showground)* **ENGLISH ECHO:** harp, violin and recorder *(in the House)* • **DANSE ROYALE:** Tudor Dancing *(West Gardens)* • **TUDOR DANCING** by Danse Royale *(South Front forecourt)* • **ENGLISH MISCELLANY:** Morris, Country and Folk dancing *(Palace Yard)* • **GUIDED TOURS OF THE GARDENS** *(start from the West Terrace)*

11am	**THE HAWK MASTER - FALCONRY ON HORSEBACK DISPLAY** *(Arena)*
12 noon	**GAMEGOER GUNDOG DISPLAY** *(Arena)*
12 noon	**TALK: 'Organic Gardening'** by David Beaumont *(East Gardens marquee)*
12 noon	**TALK: 'Tudor Dress'** by Danse Royale *(Upper Solar Room - Saturday only)*
12.45pm	**Tudor Picnic** with Danse Royale *(West Gardens - Sunday only)*
1pm	**TALK** by a Flower Tent exhibitor *(East Gardens marquee)*
1.30pm	**THE ADAMS AXEMEN DISPLAY** *(Arena - Sunday only)*
2pm	**TALK: 'Floral Design'** by Athena Tulba NAFAS *(East Gardens marquee)*
2.15pm	**GARDEN LECTURE** *(Armoury - Saturday only)*
2.30am	**THE HAWK MASTER - FALCONRY ON HORSEBACK DISPLAY** *(Arena)*
3pm	**QUESTION TIME FOR GARDENERS** *(East Gardens marquee)* Jock Davidson with a panel of experts, chaired by Lady Salisbury
3.30pm	**GAMEGOER GUNDOG DISPLAY** *(Arena)*
4pm	**TALK** by a Flower Tent exhibitor *(East Gardens marquee)*
4.15pm	**GARDEN LECTURE** *(Armoury - Saturday only)*
4.30pm	**THE ADAMS AXEMEN DISPLAY** *(Arena - Sunday only)*
4.45pm	Sale of Horticultural Exhibits *(Flower Tent - Sunday only)*
6pm	*FESTIVAL CLOSES*

Admission charges: Adult £6.80, Group (20+) £5.80, Child £3.40.
All enquiries to: The Curator's Office, Hatfield House, Hatfield,
Hertfordshire AL9 5NQ Tel: 01707 262823 Fax: 01707 275719

BEDFORDSHIRE, ESSEX & HERTFORDSHIRE

Hugh Johnson, *Saling Hall Gardens*
(GREAT SALING, NR. BRAINTREE, ESSEX)

"In this dry and only gently hilly part of England, gardeners have to work hard for effect. The best gardens use such resources as streams and springs to create sheltered oases, often in contrast to their surroundings. Famous examples include Hatfield House and Benington Lordship Garden in Hertfordshire, the Gibberd Garden at Harlow and Beth Chatto's near Colchester."

HUGH'S FAVOURITE THREE PLANTS:
The Cricket Bat Willow, Rosa glauca, Helleborus argutifolius (Corsican hellebore)

HUGH'S GARDENING HINT:
"Your garden should be rather small, or you will have no fun at all!"

This area is a potential paradise for plants people. National collections, huge garden centres and some of the most spectacular civic displays, plus a selection of the grandest stately home gardens in England.

Serious garden lovers should make a bee-line for the Royal National Rose Society's HQ near St Albans for demonstrations and trials – and the heady splendour of 30,000 Roses. They'll be fascinated too, by the Gardening Which? demonstration gardens at Capel Manor and by the RHS's latest regional garden at Hyde Hall.

The area has cultivated some famous gardeners. John Ray, the first modern botanist was born at Black Notley in Essex in 1627. Sir Joseph Paxton, gardener and designer of the Crystal Palace, is commemorated at Milton Bryan Church. A pilgrimage to Myddelton House, home of that great amateur gardener, E.A. Bowles, is a real inspiration. And at Harlow, you can visit the garden of Sir Frederick Gibberd who designed Liverpool's Roman Catholic Cathedral and Harlow New Town.

This is an area of strong civic pride. It even boasts two of the very first "Garden Cities", Letchworth and Welwyn Garden City. You'll find impressive formal displays and more relaxed parks and woodland gardens at Colchester's Victorian Castle Park, Watford's Cheslyn Gardens, Bedford's Embankment Gardens and Bridge End Gardens in charming Saffron Walden, home of the Saffron Crocus. While at Hitchin, the Lavender Town, the Physic Garden offers a fascinating glimpse into the history of medicinal herbs.

The seaside shows are splendid, too, with great splashes of colour on the seafront at Clacton-on-Sea and floral tours round Southend-on-Sea's 1000 acres of award-winning parks and gardens.

At Hatfield House, another Beth, Elizabeth I, heard of her accession. The gardens, planted by John Tradescant in the

17th century, have been beautifully restored. On a smaller scale the Edwardian gardens of Easton Lodge, home of the 'Prince of Wales' "Darling Daisy", are currently under restoration.

In Springtime, the orchards around Tiptree are a treat, as is a cream tea complete with the famous local jam! You'll find teatime treats at nearby Layer Marney Tower, too, with its beautiful turn of the century gardens.

Why not take a tour of English gardening history? Stockwood Craft Museum has gardens representing nine centuries, Wrest Park is elegant 18th century personified. Beth Chatto created her gorgeous garden out of wasteland in the 60's.

Sir Edwin Lutyens and Gertrude Jekyll designed the fine gardens at Knebworth House. Perhaps even they would have been outfaced by the 3,000 acres of deer park and record-breaking trees at Woburn Abbey. Head from here to Whipsnade and marvel at the village's Tree Cathedral. Other unusual sights, worth a detour, are the 18th century gazebos on the river at Ware and the shell-covered Scott's Grotto. There's more Victorian quaintness at the unique Swiss Garden at Old Warden with its tiny thatched buildings and grotto, while the turf maze at Saffron Walden is a pure prehistoric puzzle.

On the following pages you will find information about many of the region's gardens, including contact details, directions, special features and facilities available. Shown below is a key to the symbols used on the entries. A map reference has been provided; to be used with the map on pages 94-95. Prices shown are Adults/OAP's/Children. We do advise that you contact the individual gardens before visiting, to check opening times and admission prices as changes do occur after press date.

Saling Hall, Essex

KEY TO SYMBOLS

- ❁ Member of the East of England Tourist Board
- 🛍 gift shop
- ⚘ plants/produce for sale
- 🅿 parking
- [wc] toilet facilities
- ☕ light refreshments/snacks
- 🛋 picnic area
- ✕ restaurant/tearoom
- 𝑘 pre-booked guided tours/talks
- 🐕 dogs permitted on lead
- ♿ disabled visitors welcome
- SE special events
- 🔲 connection to famous gardener

✤ AMPTHILL

AMPTHILL PARK, *B9*
WOBURN ROAD, AMPTHILL
TEL: 01525 404355 - Ampthill Town Council

Henry VIII's favourite hunting seat, this former deer park is set on the Greensand Ridge, and was landscaped by Capability Brown around 1770. Spectacular views and walks. **Features:** Landscaped parkland. **G** - Capability Brown. Gothic cross marks site of 15th century castle, where Catherine of Aragon stayed pending her divorce. *Open: All year, daily, any reasonable time. Admission free.* **P** ⬛ *(nearby)* � ↑ ♿

KINGS ARMS PATH GARDEN, *B9*
KINGS ARMS YARD, AMPTHILL
TEL: 01525 402030 - The Friends of the Garden
From A507/A5120 - into Ampthill Old Market Square, then down Kings Arms Yard.

Secret woodland garden, created between 1968-86 by the late plantsman William Nourish. Many rare trees, shrubs, bulbs and interesting collections. Special collection of Snowdrops, Hemerocallis, Ilex, Viburnum, Hellebores, perennial Geraniums. **Features:** Arboretum and herbaceous borders. Water and woodland gardens. *Open: 13 Feb, 1400-1600. 23 Apr; 28 May; 18 Jun; 27 Aug and 22 Oct, 1430-1700. £1/£1/25p.* ❀ **P** ♴ ♿ *(wood chip paths)*

✤ BEDFORD

◎ **BEDFORD BUTTERFLY PARK,** *B7*
RENHOLD ROAD, WILDEN,
NR. BEDFORD MK44 2PX
TEL: 01234 772770 FAX: 01234 772773
From A421 - follow signs to Wilden.

Set amongst wildflower Hay meadows, hedgerows and butterfly gardens, the park features a heated glasshouse filled with luxurious tropical plants and free-flying tropical butterflies. **Features:** Rapunzel inspired summer house, herbaceous borders. Landscaped parkland and tropical house. Wildflower garden. *Open: Mar to Nov, daily, 1000-1700 £4/£3/£2.50.* ⚇ **P** ⬛ ⚱ ⚛ ✗ ♴ ♿

◎ **THE EMBANKMENT GARDENS,** *B8*
BEDFORD TEL: 01234 215226
Follow A6 into Bedford, then left on to The Embankment.

The traditional formal Victorian gardens provide a colourful array of flowers and foliage along one of England's finest river settings. Elegant suspension bridge. *Open: All year, daily, any reasonable time. Admission free.* **P** ⬛ ⚱ ⚇ ✗ ♞ ↑ ♿ SE - 27, 28 May

✤ BOLNHURST (nr. Bedford) *B7*

STABLES CHRISTIAN CENTRE,
OLD RECTORY, BOLNHURST,
NR. BEDFORD MK44 2ES
TEL: 01234 376237 FAX: 01234 376396
Six miles north of Bedford, on the B660 (Kimbolton road).

Five acres, including woodland walk and small herb garden. Over 100 varieties of herbs and wild flowers for sale. Coffee shop with home-made cakes. **Features:** Arboretum. Fruit and vegetable, herb, kitchen, scent, water, wildflower and woodland gardens *Open: 1 Apr to 31 Oct, Sat, 1430-1700. Herb sales at other times by appointment. Admission free.* ⚇ ✿ **P** ⬛ ⚱ ✗ ♞

✤ CLOPHILL *B9*

RURAL CRAFT CENTRE, SHEFFORD
ROAD, CLOPHILL MK45 4BT
TEL: 01525 860740/861366
Off the A6, at the far end of Clophill village.

Floral craft centre with a wide collection of dried and silk flowers, basketware, gift/craft shop with tea room, adventure playground, picnic area and Summer fruit picking. **Features:** Fruit, vegetable and kitchen garden. *Open: All year, daily, 1030-1700. Craft shop & tea room Wed-Sun 1000-1700. Admission free.* ⚇ ✿ **P** ⬛ ⚱ ↑ ✗ ♞ ↑ ♿

✤ LUTON *B10*

◎ **STOCKWOOD CRAFT MUSEUM AND**
GARDENS, STOCKWOOD COUNTRY
PARK, FARLEY HILL, LUTON LU1 4BH
TEL: 01582 738714 FAX: 01582 546763
From M1 (junction 10), via London Road, Whitehill Avenue and Farley Hill - to Stockwood.

Beautifully recreated period gardens tracing nine centuries of English gardening history, beginning with our Medieval Garden. Situated, in what were the walled and pleasure gardens of Stockwood House, they also include knot and Italian gardens, and offer something for every gardener

right throughout the year. **Features:** Herbaceous borders, landscaped parkland and statuary/sculpture (Ian Hamilton Finlay). Dutch, Italian, knot, rose and medieval gardens. *Open: Apr to Oct, Tues-Sat, 1000-1700; Sun, 1000-1800. Nov to Mar, Sat and Sun only, 1000-1600. Admission free.* ♿ 🅿 ᵂᶜ 🍴 ⊟ ✕ ⚐ ♿

⊛ **WARDOWN PARK,** *B10*
OLD BEDFORD ROAD, LUTON LU2 7HA
TEL: 01582 546739 FAX: 01582 546763
One mile north of the town centre, off the Old Bedford Road.

A large public park, with woodland garden and herbaceous borders. Museum, tennis courts, boating lake and children's playground. **Features:** Herbaceous borders and landscaped parkland. Woodland garden. *Open: All year, daily, any reasonable time. Admission free.* 🅿 ᵂᶜ 🍴 ⊟ 🐕 ♿

✢ **OLD WARDEN** *(nr. Biggleswade)* *C8*
⊛ **THE SWISS GARDEN,**
OLD WARDEN PARK, OLD WARDEN,
NR. BIGGLESWADE SG18 9EA
TEL: 01767 627666 FAX: 01767 627443
Entrance in Old Warden village - 3 miles west of the A1 at Biggleswade.

Laid out in the early 1800's, this romantic and unique landscape garden is a fairytale place set within Old Warden Park, and approached via the elegant Shuttleworth Mansion. The garden contains tiny thatched buildings, bridges, ponds and a spectacular grotto/fernery. Majestic trees and acres of flowering shrubs and old climbing roses. **Features:** Garden folly (grotto and fernery). Rock/alpine and woodland gardens. *Open: Mar to Sept, Mon-Sat, 1300-1800; Sun and Bank Hols, 1000-1800. Jan, Feb and Oct, Sundays only. 1100-1500. £3/£2/£2.* ♿ ☕ 🅿 ᵂᶜ 🍴 ⊟ ✕ ⚐ ♿ SE - 14 May

✢ **SANDY** *C8*
⊛ **RSPB THE LODGE RESERVE,**
SANDY SG19 2DL
TEL: 01767 680541 FAX: 01767 683508
From the A1 - pass through the town of Sandy, on the B1042 (Potton road).

Beautiful natural gardens run on organic methods on nature reserve with specimen trees, herbaceous borders with wildlife garden and large pool. **Features:** Arboretum and herbaceous borders. Wildlife garden, woodland and water gardens. **G** - Henry Doubleday. *Open 0900-1715 weekdays, 1000-1715 Sat, Sun, Bank Hols. £2.50/£1.50/50p.* ♿ 🅿 ᵂᶜ 🍴 ⊟ ⚐ ♿

✢ **SILSOE** *(nr. Luton)* *B9*
⊛ **WREST PARK GARDENS**
(English Heritage), WREST PARK,
SILSOE, NR. LUTON MK45 4HS
TEL: 01525 860152
Three quarters of a mile east of Silsoe, off the A6 (ten miles south of Bedford).

One hundred and fifty years of English garden. Over ninety acres of wonderful design gardens include The Great Garden, with its charming buildings; the Orangery, Bath House and Archer Pavilion; the Longwater and Leg O' Mutton Lake and ornaments, alongside the intricate French Garden. **Features:** Landscaped parkland. Parterre and rose gardens. *Open: 1 Apr to 31 Oct, Sat, Sun and Bank Hols, 1000-1800 (1700 in October). Last admission at 1700 (1600 in Oct) £3.40/£2.60/£1.70 (includes audio tour).* ♿ 🅿 ᵂᶜ 🍴 ⊟ 🐕 ♿ SE - May

Sir Joseph Paxton (1803-1865)

Sir Joseph was born into a poor farming family at Milton Bryan in Bedfordshire. He received little education, but rose to become a famous English gardener and architect. He was the first person in Britain to flower the giant water-lily and in 1850, he designed the Crystal Palace for the Great Exhibition in Hyde Park. There is a memorial window to him in Milton Bryan's church.

✤ **WHIPSNADE** *(nr. Dunstable)*   *B10*
◎ WHIPSNADE TREE CATHEDRAL
(The National Trust),
WHIPSNADE, NR. DUNSTABLE
TEL: 01494 528051 FAX: 01494 463310
Two miles south of Dunstable, off the B4540.

Peaceful area with many species of trees planted in the traditional pattern of a cathedral, with grassy avenues for the nave and transepts. Near to Whipsnade Downs, where the Trust owns a farm and an area of botanically rich grass chalkland, to which there is restricted access on foot. *Open: All year, daily, any reasonable time. An annual service is held at the end of June, please telephone for details. Admission free.* **P** - *(Whipsnade village green or in Downs car park)*

BEDFORDSHIRE

✤ **WOBURN**   *A9*
◎ WOBURN ABBEY,
WOBURN MK43 0TP
TEL: 01525 290666 FAX: 01525 290271
Located just off the M1 (junction 12 or 13).

The gardens and 3,000 acre deer park surrounding Woburn Abbey, were designed by Repton. Many national champion trees. The Maze and private gardens are only open on certain days. **Features:** Arboretum, garden folly, herbaceous borders, landscaped parkland, maze (Hornbeam) topiary and tropical house. Wildflower garden. Special collection of Daffodils/Narcissi (over 100 varieties). **G** - Humphry Repton. *Open: Mar to Sept, daily, 1100-1600 (1700 on Sun and Bank Hols). House, gardens and grounds - £7.50/£6.50/£3. Park and gardens only - £5 per car (including occupants) (1999 prices).* ♿ ♣ **P** **WC** ♨ ⧓ ✗ ✗ ♿ SE - 29-31 May

ESSEX

The Saffron Crocus

The picturesque town of Saffron Walden in Essex gets part of its name from one of the oldest of all cultivated flowers, the colourful Saffron Crocus (Crocus sativus). Its arrival in England is shrouded in mystery. Did the Romans bring it with them? Or did a pilgrim smuggle the Saffron corms or bulbs from the Holy Land inside his staff? However it arrived, the crocus flourished in the rich soil around the town. It was soon found that its bright orange stigmas had many uses, from medicinal remedies and the colouring of food and drink, to a dye for wool. As the town was at the centre of the great medieval wool trade, this brought much prosperity and the image of the flower was used to decorate the plasterwork of buildings and incorporated into the town's coat of arms. In the 18th century, cheaper imports caused a gradual decline in the growing of Saffron and today, only a small bed may be seen flowering outside the town's museum in late October to early November. The corms of the crocus can be obtained from the museum and Tourist Information Centre, from mid-August to mid-September, for late Autumn flowering.

✤ ABRIDGE *(nr. Loughton)*   *E12*

BBC ESSEX GARDEN, CROWTHER
NURSERIES, ONGAR ROAD, ABRIDGE,
NR. LOUGHTON RM4 1AA
TEL: 01708 688581 FAX: 01708 688677
*Two miles east of Abridge on the A113 between
Chigwell and Ongar.*

Decorative shrub beds, flower borders,
vegetable plot and two small greenhouses
(worked at weekends in the Summer). Next
door is Sheila Chapman's 450 varieties of
Clematis. **Features:** Herbaceous borders.
Special collection of Clematis Jackmamii
(by Summer 2000) 🄶 - Ken Crowther. *Open:
All year, daily, 0930-1700. Closed 25-29 Dec.
Admission free.* ⬥ ✤ 🅿 🆆 ⬛ 🎋 ✕ 🕴 ⬥ SE - Sept

✤ AUDLEY END *(nr. Saffron Walden)*   *F9*

◎ AUDLEY END HOUSE AND
GARDENS (English Heritage),
AUDLEY END,
NR. SAFFRON WALDEN CB11 4JF
TEL: 01799 522399 FAX: 01799 521276
*One mile west of Saffron Walden on the B1383
(M11 exits 8/9 northbound only, and 10)*

Built by Thomas Howard, Earl of Suffolk,
the gardens include a 19th century parterre
and Rose garden, surrounded by an 18th
century 'Capability Brown' landscaped park.
Of special interest is the recently opened
organic kitchen garden. Visitors can purchase
their own organic produce. **Features:**
Garden follies, landscaped parkland and statuary/
sculpture. Parterre and Rose gardens. 🄶 -
Lancelot 'Capability' Brown. *Gardens open:
1 Apr-30 Sept, Wed-Sun & Bank Hols, 1100-
1800. House open from 1300. Last entry 1700.
House & Gardens open in Oct, Wed-Sun, 1000-
1500. Last entry 1500. House and gardens
£6.50/£4.90/£3.30/£16.30 (family ticket).
Gardens and grounds only - £4.50/£3.40/£2.30/
£11.30 (family ticket).* ⬥ ✤ 🅿 🆆 ⬛ 🎋 ✕ 🕴 🐾 ⬥
(ground floor of house and grounds). SE - 29, 30
Apr & 1 May, 26, 27, 28 Aug.

✤ BLACKMORE END *(nr. Braintree)*   *G9*

ELMS FARM, BLACKMORE END,
NR. BRAINTREE CM7 4DB
TEL: 01371 815218
*From Braintree, take B1053 to Wethersfield. Turn
right in the village, and follow unclassified road
towards Sible Hedingham. After one mile, turn
right again to Blackmore End.*

Lovely country garden with old roses (many
rare), and dry/water gardens. **Features:**
Arboretum. Italian, Rose, water, knot, scent,
sunken and wildflower gardens. National
Collection of Rosa Bourboniana, (Bourbon).
Special collection of Paeony. *Open: During the
month of Jun only, daily, 1130-1600. At other
times by appointment only. £1.50 (proceeds to
N.C.C.P.G. and Royal National Rose Society).*
⬥ ✤ 🅿 🆆 ⬛ 🎋 🐾 ⬥

✤ BOXTED *(nr. Colchester)*

CARTER'S VINEYARDS,   *I9*
GREEN LANE, BOXTED,
NR. COLCHESTER CO4 5TS
TEL: 01206 271136 FAX: 01206 271136
*From A134 (just after passing Gt. Horkesley), turn
right into Boxted Church Road. Then take the
second turning on your right into Green Lane.*

Forty acres of lakes, woodland and vines.
Tours of the winery and wine tastings available.
The whole enterprise is powered by alternative
energy. Wildlife nature trail. **Features:**
Landscaped parkland and vineyard. *Open:
Easter to end Sept, daily, 1100-1700. £2.50/£2.50/
free (includes wine-tasting).* ✤ 🅿 🆆 ⬛ 🎋 🐾 ⬥

THE COTTAGE GARDEN,   *I9*
LANGHAM ROAD,
BOXTED, COLCHESTER
CO4 5HU
TEL: 01206 272269
*A134 (North). Right to Boxted, 1st left Langham
Road. At the bottom on left.*

Individual nursery in garden setting featuring
a wide selection of plants, trees and shrubs,
garden antiques, interesting garden gifts
and other artefacts. **Features:** Herbaceous
borders, statuary/sculpture collection. Herb
garden. Special collection of hardy perennial
geraniums. *Open: Mar-Aug 0800-1730 daily.
Sept-Feb 0800-1600, closed Tues & Wed.
Admission free.* See Display Ad Page (Page 84).
⬥ ✤ 🅿 🆆 ⬥

✤ BRAINTREE *G10*
JOHN RAY GARDEN, BRAINTREE AND BOCKING PUBLIC GARDENS, BOCKING END, BRAINTREE
TEL: 01376 550066 - Braintree Tourist Information Centre
Located in the town centre.

A knot garden planted to commemorate John Ray (founder of the modern study of botany), with plants and flowers known to have been growing in England at the end of the 17th century. **Features:** Herb, knot and Rose gardens. *Open: All year, daily, any reasonable time. Admission free.* **P** *(nearby)*

✤ CASTLE HEDINGHAM
(nr. Halstead) *H9*
◎ HEDINGHAM CASTLE, CASTLE HEDINGHAM, NR. HALSTEAD CO9 3DJ
TEL: 01787 460261 FAX: 01787 461473
On the B1058, one mile off the A1017 (between Cambridge and Colchester).

Hedingham Castle is one of the best preserved Norman keeps in England. It was built in 1140, and was home to the de Veres, the Earls of Oxford. There are lovely walks in the peaceful woodland surrounding the castle, with a collection of rare and unusual trees and plants, in a natural setting. **Features:** Landscaped parkland. Water and woodland gardens. Special collection of snowdrops. *Open: Easter to Oct, daily, 1000-1700. Special open days in Feb/Mar to view Snowdrops £3.50/£3.00/£2.50.* ♨ ❀ **P** **wc** ♨ ⦿ ✗ ⚲ ⦿ SE - telephone for details

✤ CHELMSFORD

CENTRAL PARK, BELL MEADOW AND SKY BLUE PASTURE *G11*
TEL: 01245 606610 FAX: 01245 606970
Adjacent to Bellmead and Parkway. Close to town centre.

Attractively landscaped areas. During the Spring and Summer there are numerous floral displays with golden themed planting and carpet bedding sculpture. **Features:** Herbaceous borders and landscaped parkland. Rose and scent gardens, golden anniversary memorial garden. *Open all year round. Admission free.* **wc** ⦿ ⚲ ⦿

◎ HYLANDS PARK, CHELMSFORD *G11*
TEL: 01245 606812 FAX: 01245 606970
Access to the park (in normal opening hours) is from the A414 (Chelmsford to Harlow road) and A1016 (follow brown signs).

Hylands Park extends to some 600 acres, and includes a partially restored Grade II* neo-classical mansion, ornamental pleasure gardens, lakes and woodland. The House is open Sundays, Mondays, and Bank Holidays. Some of the parkland was designed by the famous landscape gardener Humphry Repton. **Features:** Ornamental rose and herbaceous terrace (1900 style). Arboretum, garden folly (flint cottage), landscaped parkland. Dell and ornamental lily ponds. **G** - Humphry Repton. A special events programme runs throughout the year. *Open: All year, daily, from 0730 (closes half an hour after dusk). Access maybe limited during certain events. Admission free (to park and gardens).* **P** **wc** ⦿ *(Suns only, all year round),* ⦿ ⚲ ⦿ SE - throughout year, please contact Linda Pittom for details (01245 606812).

❂ OAKLANDS PARK,   *G11*
MOULSHAM STREET, CHELMSFORD
TEL: 01245 606610 FAX: 01245 606970
From Princes Road, turn left into Moulsham
Street and follow brown road signs.

The grounds cover some twelve acres, and contains the Chelmsford and Essex Museum and the Essex Regiment Museum. Ornamental gardens and lawns, children's play facilities, tennis courts and football pitch. **Features:** Herbaceous borders and landscaped parkland. Walled flower garden. Rose and fern gardens. Tree collection. Special collections of Camellia, Helleborus, Hosta, Jasmine, Magnolia, Mediterranean plants and Viburnum. *Open: All year, daily, from 0730 (closes half an hour after dusk). Admission free.* **P** 🅦 🏞 🐾 ♿

❂ TOWER GARDENS,   *G11*
RAINSFORD ROAD, CHELMSFORD
TEL: 01245 606610 FAX: 01245 606970
Located half a mile from Chelmsford town centre, along Rainsford Road.

Tower Gardens comprises of five acres, including formal gardens, bowling green, tennis courts and access to riverside walks. **Features:** Garden folly (conduit) and herbaceous borders. Tree collection. *Open: All year, daily, from 0730 (closes half an hour after dusk). Admission free.* 🏞 🐾 ♿

✤ CLACTON-ON-SEA   *J/K10*
❂ CLACTON'S SEAFRONT GARDENS, MARINE PARADE WEST, CLACTON-ON-SEA
From A133 proceed to seafront, gardens can be found on Marine Parade West.

Memorial gardens, stretching along seafront (parallel to Marine Parade West). Extensive refurbishment during 1999. Good displays of bedding plants and annuals, best seen in Summer. **Features:** Sunken garden. *Open: All year, daily, any reasonable time. Admission free.* **P** *(nearby)*

✤ COLCHESTER

❂ CASTLE PARK,   *I10*
HIGH STREET, COLCHESTER
TEL: 01206 282920 FAX: 01206 282924
From the town centre, follow pedestrian signs for Colchester Castle Museum (which is situated in Castle Park).

Castle Park is an oasis of horticultural splendour, and a delight for the senses all year round. But it is not just popular with visitors for its gardens - this award-winning Victorian park is the setting for Europe's largest Norman keep, and the gentle slopes provide the perfect venue for fairs, festivals and open air concerts. **Features:** Victorian parkland with 18th century landscaping influences, large collection of trees, garden folly. Mixed herbaceous and shrub gardens; rose, sensory and sunken gardens. Magnificent bedding and bulb displays. *Open: All year, daily, 0730 until dusk. Admission free.* 🅦 🏞 ⚘ 🐾 *(in Lower Castle Park only)* ♿

❂ TYMPERLEYS,   *I10*
TRINITY STREET, COLCHESTER
TEL: 01206 282920   FAX: 01206 282924
From High Street, walk down Pelham's Lane, turn right, then first left into Trinity Street.

Tymperleys, a magnificent 15th Century, timber framed house, is now a clock museum. Its garden is a superb example of a town centre courtyard garden with Elizabethan themed planting. **Features:** Herbaceous borders. Herb garden. *Open: Apr to Oct, Tues - Sat. Closed 1300-1400. Admission free.* ♿

✤ COGGESHALL *H9/10*

⊛ MARKS HALL ESTATE AND
ARBORETUM, ESTATE OFFICE,
MARKS HALL, COGGESHALL CO6 1TG
TEL: 01376 563769 FAX: 01376 563132
*Follow the brown tourist signs, from the A120 at
Coggeshall.*

Ancient woodlands form a backdrop to this
historic estate, which has a new arboretum,
ornamental lakes, cascades, walled garden,
parkland and mature avenues. Facilities for
the disabled. Programme of events, shop,
cafe and visitor centre. **Features:** Arboretum
and landscaped parkland. *Open: Arboretum/visitor
centre - Easter to 31 Oct, Tues-Fri, 1030-1630; Sat,
Sun and Bank Hols, 1030-1800. Car park, woodland walks and picnic site open all year. £3 per car.*
♿ ♻ 🅿 ♨ ⚌ 🍴 ✗ ✗ 🐾 (outside arboretum) ♿
SE - 7 May

⊛ PAYCOCKES *H10*
(The National Trust), WEST STREET,
COGGESHALL CO6 1NS
TEL: 01376 561305 FAX: 01376 561305
*Signposted off the A120 on south side of West
Street (about 300m from centre of Coggeshall).*

A merchant's house dating from c.1500, and
containing rich panelling and wood carving.
Displays of Coggeshall lace. Lovely cottage-
style garden. **Features:** Herbaceous
borders. Kitchen garden. *Open: 2 Apr to 15 Oct,
Tues, Thurs, Sun and Bank Hol Mon, 1400-1730*

*(last admission 1700). £2.20/£1.20/£3 (joint ticket
with the nearby National Trust property of Grange
Barn).* 🅿 *(at Grange Barn)* ✗

✤ CRESSING *(nr. Braintree)* *H10*
⊛ CRESSING TEMPLE,
WITHAM ROAD, CRESSING,
NR. BRAINTREE CM7 8PD
TEL: 01376 584903 FAX: 01376 584864
*Located off the B1018, between Witham and
Braintree.*

Tudor walled garden, recreated from
extensive research in the 'paradisal style'.
Features: Garden folly (arbour and
fountain), herbaceous borders and vineyard.
Herb, kitchen (potager), knot, parterre,
scent (nosegay) and wildflower (flowery
mead) gardens. Early vegetables and dyers
plants. *Open: Sun, Mar-Oct, Wed, Thurs, Fri,
May-Sept, daily, 1030-1730. £3/£2/£2.* ♿ ♻ 🅿 ⚌
🍴 🍽 ✗ ✗ 🐾 ♿ SE - Apr/May

✤ ELMSTEAD MARKET
(nr. Colchester) *J10*
THE BETH CHATTO GARDENS LIMITED,
ELMSTEAD MARKET,
NR. COLCHESTER CO7 7DB
TEL: 01206 822007 FAX: 01206 825933
Quarter of a mile east of Elmstead Market, on the A133.

Wonderful landscaped gardens, with many
unusual plants shown in different conditions.
From dry gravel areas filled with drought
resistant plants, to dramatic water and
woodland gardens. **Features:** Herbaceous
borders, alpine, water, woodland and 'drought-
resistant' gravel gardens. 🅖 - Beth Chatto.
*Open: 1 Mar to 31 Oct, Mon-Sat, 0900-1700.
1 Nov to 28/29 Feb, Mon-Fri, 0900-1600. Closed
Sun and Bank Hols. £3/£3/free.* ♻ 🅿 ⚌ 🍴

✤ FEERING *(nr. Colchester)* *H10*
FEERINGBURY MANOR,
COGGESHALL ROAD, FEERING,
NR. COLCHESTER CO5 9RB
TEL: 01376 561946
*On the unclassified road between Coggeshall and
Feering, (not Kelvedon).*

An ebullient six acre garden, packed with
rare and interesting plants for damp and
dry areas. Interesting modern sculpture and
gates, add to the pleasure. Old-fashioned
roses. **Features:** Garden folly (arbour),
herbaceous borders and statuary/sculpture.
Water gardens and woodland gardens.
🅖 - Cedric Morris. *Open: Thur, Fri 0800-1600,
4 May to 28 Jul 2000. £2/£2/free.* 🅿 ⚌ *(not disabled)*
⚌ *(prebooked)* 🍴 🐾 ♿ SE - contact for details

✣ **FELSTED** *(nr. Great Dunmow)* G10
FELSTED VINEYARDS,
CRIX GREEN, FELSTED,
NR. GREAT DUNMOW CM6 3JT
TEL: 01245 361504 FAX: 01245 361504
Two miles behind the Essex Showground (A131) - follow signs.

East Anglia's oldest commercial vineyard, producing fine English wines - well worth a visit! **Features:** Vineyard. *Open: Easter to Oct, daily, 1000-1800. Closed Mon (except Bank Hols). Admission free.* ♿ ❀ **P** **WC** ⌂ 🍴 🐕 🐾 ♿

✣ **GREAT SALING** *(nr. Braintree)* G9/10
SALING HALL GARDEN,
GREAT SALING,
NR. BRAINTREE CM7 5DT
TEL: 01371 850243 FAX: 01371 850274
Turn north off the A120 between Braintree and Dunmow at the Saling Oak pub.

Twelve acres with walled garden, fish ponds and small park with fine collection of unusual trees. **Features:** Arboretum, garden folly (Temple of Pisces), herbaceous borders, landscaped parkland and statuary/sculpture. Herb, kitchen, Japanese, scent, water, wildflower, woodland and shrub gardens. Special collections of Quercus, Sorbus and Pines. **G** - Hugh Johnson. *Open: May, Jun and Jul, Wed, 1400-1700 (in aid of the National Gardens Scheme). £2/£2/free.* **P** **WC** ♿

✣ **GREAT WALTHAM**
(nr. Chelmsford) G10/11
PARK FARM, CHATHAM HALL LANE,
GREAT WALTHAM,
NR. CHELMSFORD CM3 1BZ
TEL: 01245 360871
Take B1008 north from Chelmsford, turn left into lane signposted 'Howe Street'.

Two acres of garden in separate 'rooms' formed by Yew hedges, with climber-obscured old farmhouse and dairy in centre. Bulbs, shrubs and perennials. Designing still proceeding. **Features:** Rose and water gardens. *Open: 9, 10, 23, 24, 30 Apr; 1, 14, 15, 28, 29 May; 11, 12, 25, 26 Jun; 9, 10 Jul.* ❀ **P** **WC** ☕ ⚱

✣ **HARLOW** E11
THE GIBBERD GARDEN,
MARSH LANE, GILDEN WAY,
HARLOW CM17 0NA
TEL: 01279 442112
Take B183 from Harlow (east). Narrow left turning after one mile (approx.)

20th century garden, designed by Sir Frederick Gibberd, sloping to small river. Wild garden, moated "castle", pools, "Roman Temple", collection of modern sculpture. **Features:** Garden folly (gazebo, "Roman Temple", moated "castle" and statuary/sculpture. Water and woodland gardens. **G** - Sir Frederick Gibberd. *Open: Sats and Suns from Easter Sun to end of Sept, 1400-1800. £3/£2/free.* ❀ **P** **WC** ⚱ ✕ 🍴 🐕 🐾 ♿

✣ **HARLOW** E11
MARK HALL GARDENS,
MUSKHAM ROAD,
HARLOW CM20 2LF
TEL: 01279 446997/439680
FAX: 01279 453950/442786
Signposted from the A414 - 300yds from junction with First Avenue in Harlow.

Attractive plantsman's garden based on three themes - unusual fruits, 17th century herb and parterres and large walled garden, featuring cottage plants, Roses and Winter borders. **Features:** Herbaceous borders and statuary/sculpture. Fruit and vegetable, herb, kitchen, parterre and Rose gardens. *Open: Mon-Fri, 1000-1500; Sun, 1100-1530. Closed on Sat. Admission free.* **P** **WC** ♿

✣ **HORNCHURCH** F12
NEW ZEALAND AND AUSTRALIAN
PLANTS, COUNTY PARK NURSERY,
ESSEX GARDENS,
HORNCHURCH RM11 3BU
TEL: 01708 445205
From M25 (junction 29), take A127 towards London. After two and a half miles, turn left into Wingletye Lane, then left again into Essex Gardens.

Small plantsman's nursery, with large variety of unusual and rare plants on display. **Features:** Garden folly (grotto). National Collections of Coprosma and Parahebe. Special collections of Podocarpus, Pittosporum, Carmichaelia and Hebe. *Open: Apr to Oct, Mon-Sat (closed on Wed), 0900-1800; Sun, 1000-1700. Nov to Mar, by appointment only. Admission free.* ❀ **P** *(on road)*

ESSEX

✢ LAYER MARNEY (nr. Colchester) I10

◎ LAYER MARNEY TOWER,
LAYER MARNEY,
NR. COLCHESTER CO5 9US
TEL: 01206 330784 FAX: 01206 330784
Signposted off the B1022 (Colchester to Maldon road), near the town of Tiptree.

Tallest Tudor gatehouse in the country, with a lovely formal garden. Medieval barn with rare breed farm animals. Beautiful pond, recently planted with Roses and wildflowers. **Features:** Landscaped parkland. Rose garden. *Open: 1 Apr to 6 Oct, daily (except Sat), 1100-1700. £3.25/£3.25/£1.75.* 🕮 ❀ 🅿 WC ♨ 🍴 ✗ 🥾 🐕 ᵼ SE

✢ LEIGH-ON-SEA H12/13

◎ BELFAIRS PARK AND NATURE RESERVE, EASTWOOD ROAD NORTH, LEIGH-ON-SEA
TEL: 01702 215610 - Parks Dept,
Southend Council FAX: 01702 215631
From A13, turn left into Eastwood Road, then left again into Eastwood Road North.

Outdoor sports facilities, gardens, walks (set in woodlands) and a nature reserve containing ancient woodland, home to many species of flora and fauna. **Features:** Landscaped parkland. Woodland garden. *Open: All year, daily, from 0730 (closing times subject to seasonal variations). Admission free.* 🅿 WC ♨ ✗ 🐕

✢ LITTLE EASTON (nr. Great Dunmow) F10

THE GARDENS OF EASTON LODGE,
WARWICK HOUSE, EASTON LODGE,
LITTLE EASTON,
NR. GREAT DUNMOW CM6 2BB
TEL: 01371 876979 FAX: 01371 876979
Off the B184 (Gt. Dunmow to Thaxted road) - follow brown tourist signs.

Twenty acre garden with pergolas, terraces, pools, pavilions, lawns, trees, shrubs and flowers, including thousands of snowdrops at Springtime. Harold Peto's 'Italian Gardens' are currently being restored. Visit the exhibition in the dovecote. Picnic by the Lily pond, in the newly restored pavilion or down in the glade, site of the Japanese gardens. **Features:** Garden folly (two pavilions) and herbaceous borders. Dell Glade Italian, Rose, water, wildflower and woodland gardens. 🄶 - Harold Peto's. *Open: Easter to the end of Oct, Fri, Sat, Sun and Bank Hol Mon, 1200-1800. Other times by appointment only. Special openings during Feb and Mar for Snowdrop displays. £3.30/£3/£1 (over 3yrs).* ❀ 🅿 WC ♨ 🍴 ᵼ 🥾 🐕 SE - Easter.

LITTLE EASTON MANOR GARDENS, F10
PARK ROAD, LITTLE EASTON,
NR. GREAT DUNMOW CM6 2JN
TEL: 01371 872857 FAX: 01371 878479
Off the B184 (Gt. Dunmow to Thaxted road), signposted Little Easton. Take first left, and follow road for one mile. Situated next to church.

The manor grounds include acres of lawns, parterre, topiary and lakes, with fountains and wildlife. Wheelchair pathways, and free deck chairs. Tea rooms. **Features:** Garden folly (two gazebos), herbaceous borders, statuary/sculpture and topiary. Fruit and vegetable, herb, kitchen and parterre gardens. *Open: First Thurs in Jun, 1400-1700, & every Thurs until end Sept. £2/£2/free.* ❀ 🅿 WC ♨ 🍴 ✗ ᵼ 🐕 🥾 SE - throughout the year.

✢ MALDON H11

MALDON MILLENNIUM GARDEN,
ST. PETER'S CHURCHYARD,
MARKET HILL, MALDON CM9 4PZ
TEL: 01621 857373 FAX: 01621 850793
Located in the town centre.

A representation of a 10th century garden, containing monastic and wild herbal gardens - needs to be seen as a whole garden. Quiet oasis. **Features:** Fruit and vegetable, herb and wildflower gardens. *Open: All year, daily, any reasonable time. Admission free.* 🅿 *(nearby)*

✢ NAYLAND (nr. Colchester) I9

LOWER DAIRY HOUSE GARDEN,
WATER LANE, NAYLAND,
NR. COLCHESTER CO6 4JS
TEL: 01206 262220 FAX: 01206 263574
Signposted off the A134 (Colchester to Bury St Edmunds road). Half a mile up Water Lane.

Plantsman's garden, designed for all year round colour, with mass planting in a

80

cont. next page.

cottage garden style. Stream, rockeries, pond and borders. **Features:** Herbaceous borders. Dell, fruit and vegetable, herb, kitchen, rock/alpine, Rose, scent, water and wildflower gardens. *Open: 9, 16, 23, 24, 30 Apr, 1, 7, 14, 21, 28, 29 May; 4, 11, 18, 25 Jun; 2, 9 Jul, 1400-1800. £2/£2/50p.* ♨ P � &

✢ **PURLEIGH** *(nr. Chelmsford)* H11
NEW HALL VINEYARDS,
CHELMSFORD ROAD, PURLEIGH,
NR. CHELMSFORD CM3 6PN
TEL: 01621 828343 FAX: 01621 828343
Situated on the B1010 to Burnham on Crouch.

Guided tours of the vineyards, with a trail through the vines and cellars where wine can be tasted. Also visit the press house with slide shows. See fermentation and bottling. **Features:** Vineyard. *Open: All year, Mon-Fri, 1000-1700; Sat and Sun, 1000-1330. Admission free.* ♨ P � ✗ ♠ & SE - 22, 23 Aug

✢ **RETTENDON** *(nr. Chelmsford)* G11/12
◎ THE ROYAL HORTICULTURAL
SOCIETY'S GARDEN 'HYDE HALL',
RETTENDON, NR. CHELMSFORD CM3 8ET
TEL: 01245 400256 FAX: 01245 402100
Follow the brown tourist signs from the A130 at The Bell Inn (Rettendon).

An eight acre garden with herbaceous borders, Roses and ornamental ponds. This is a major regional garden in the making. 2000 will see a new rose garden and new gardens in the Malus field. **Features:** Arboretum, herbaceous borders, landscaped parkland and tropical house. Dell, rock/alpine, Rose, sunken, water and woodland gardens. National Collection of Viburnum. Special collection of Roses and Waterlilies. *Open: End Mar to end Aug, daily, 1100-1800 (1700 in Sept and Oct) £3/£3/70p (6-16yrs).* ♿ ♨ P � ⚊ ⊓ ✗ ♠ *(guide dogs only)* &

✢ **SAFFRON WALDEN**

◎ BRIDGE END GARDENS, F8/9
BRIDGE STREET, SAFFRON WALDEN
TEL: 01799 510445 - Saffron Walden
Tourist Information Centre
FAX: 01799 510445
From Cambridge on the B184, turn left into Castle Street - follow brown tourist signs.

Restored Victorian gardens created mostly during the 1840s. **Features:** Garden folly (gazebo), herbaceous borders, landscaped parkland, maze (Yew hedge) and statuary/sculpture. Dutch, fruit and vegetable, kitchen and Rose gardens. *Open: All year, daily, any reasonable time. Entrance (and key) to the maze and kitchen garden, is by prior arrangement only, with the Tourist Information Centre. Admission free.* P *(nearby)* � ⊓ ♠

SAFFRON WALDEN TURF MAZE, F8/9
THE COMMON, SAFFRON WALDEN
TEL: 01799 510444 - Saffron Walden
Tourist Information Centre
In the centre of the town, at the eastern end of the Common.

Largest surviving turf maze in England, at about hundred feet (thirty metres) in diameter. First recorded in 1699, it was used in some form of fertility rite to ensure a good harvest. **Features:** Maze (turf). *Open: All year, daily, any reasonable time. Admission free.* P *(nearby)* � ♠ &

John Ray (1627-1705)
John Ray is regarded as the father of natural history. He was born and lived most of his life in the village of Black Notley in Essex. Ray's greatest work, the three-volume 'Historia Plantaraum' (History of Plants) 1686-1704, describes and classifies over 1800 kinds of plants. The 300th anniversary of this great work was celebrated in 1986, with the creation of a traditional knot garden, planted with flowers known to have been growing in this country by the end of the 17th century. You can find it at the public gardens at Braintree/Bocking.

⊹ SOUTHEND-ON-SEA

◎ CHURCHILL GARDENS, *H12/13*
EAST STREET, SOUTHEND-ON-SEA
TEL: 01702 215610 - Parks Dept,
Southend Council FAX: 01702 215631
Take the A127 to Victoria Avenue, then turn left into East Street, at the traffic lights.

Secluded ornamental gardens, with a waterfall and stream fringed with bog and shrub planting. Areas of lawn provide opportunities for quiet contemplation. **Features:** Landscaped parkland. Water garden. *Open: All year, daily, from 0730 (closing times subject to seasonal variations). Admission free.* 🐎 &

◎ CLIFFTOP GARDENS, *H12/13*
SOUTHEND-ON-SEA
TEL: 01702 215610 - Parks Dept,
Southend Council FAX: 01702 215631
From the A127, follow the brown tourist signs to the Bandstand.

The Clifftop Gardens are renowned for their Spring and Summer bedding displays, which stretch for over a kilometre along the seafront, affording spectacular views over the Thames estuary. **Features:** Landscaped parkland. Rock/alpine garden. *Open: All year, daily, any reasonable time. Admission free.* 🐎

◎ PRIORY PARK, *H12/13*
VICTORIA AVENUE,
SOUTHEND-ON-SEA
TEL: 01702 215610 - Parks Dept,
Southend Council FAX: 01702 215631
From the A127, follow the brown tourist signs for 'Prittlewell Priory Museum'.

Built around a 12th century Cluniac monastery, Priory Park features ornamental gardens, seasonal bedding displays, a fishing lake and sporting facilities. **Features:** Herbaceous borders, landscaped parkland, herb, rock/alpine, Rose and water gardens. *Open: All year, daily, from 0730 (closing times subject to seasonal variations). Admission free.* 🅿 ♿ 🚻 ☕ ⛱ ✕ 🐎 &

◎ PRITTLEWELL SQUARE, *H12/13*
CLIFFTOWN PARADE,
SOUTHEND-ON-SEA
TEL: 01702 215610 - Parks Dept,
Southend Council FAX: 01702 215631
From the A127, follow the brown tourist signs to the 'Cliffs Bandstand'. Prittlewell Square is opposite.

As Southend's oldest public park (dating back to 1855), Prittlewell Square with its peaceful setting has a formal central pond with fountains, and is surrounded by flowerbeds and lawns. **Features:** Scent garden. *Open: All year, daily, any reasonable time. Admission free.* 🐎 &

◎ SOUTHCHURCH HALL GARDENS, *H12/13*
WOODGRANGE DRIVE,
SOUTHEND-ON-SEA
TEL: 01702 215610 - Parks Dept,
Southend Council FAX: 01702 215631
From the A127, follow the brown tourist signs to the 'Southchurch Hall Museum'.

Ornamental gardens with large ponds containing fish and wildfowl. Set around a 13th century medieval hall, now used as a museum. **Features:** Landscaped parkland. *Open: All year, daily, from 0730 (closing times subject to seasonal variations). Admission free.* 🚻 🐎 &

◎ SOUTHCHURCH PARK, *H12/13*
NORTHUMBERLAND CRESCENT,
SOUTHEND-ON-SEA
TEL: 01702 215610 - Parks Dept,
Southend Council FAX: 01702 215631
From A1159, turn right into Southchurch Boulevard, then left into Lifstan Way. Entrance to park is second turning on right.

Gardens with shrubs, bedding displays and Roses. A boating lake, Children's play area, and a wide range of sporting facilities are also available. **Features:** Herbaceous borders and landscaped parkland. *Open: All year, daily, from 0730 (closing times subject to seasonal variations). Admission free.* 🅿 🚻 ♿ ⛱ ✕ 🐎 &

Southend-on-Sea
This popular seaside resort is famous for its award-winning parks and gardens. Most of the town's parks were established between 1900 and 1930 and cover over 1000 acres. It even boasts a nursery of twelve acres for raising plants for use within the parks. This has brought the town honours for four years running in the 'Britain in Bloom' awards, alongside gold, silver and bronze medals at the prestigious Chelsea Flower Show in 1995, 1996, 1997, 1998, and 1999. During the Summer, visitors can enjoy special guided floral tours around the main displays.

ESSEX

✤ TAKELEY (nr. Bishop's Stortford)   F10
☸ HATFIELD FOREST NATIONAL NATURE RESERVE (The National Trust), ESTATE OFFICE, TAKELEY, NR. BISHOP'S STORTFORD CM22 6NE
TEL: 01279 870678 FAX: 01279 871938
Signposted off the A120 in the village of Takeley, two miles east of junction 8 of the M11.

A rare, surviving medieval hunting forest. 1,000 acres of ancient woodland and pastures with wonderful four hundred year old pollarded trees, two ornamental lakes and an 18th century shell house. Wildflowers in Spring. **G** - Lancelot 'Capability' Brown. *Open: All year, daily. Car park charge.* **P** **WC** ☕ **Ħ** ★ 占
SE - please telephone for details.

✤ WALTHAM ABBEY

☸ ABBEY GARDENS,   E11
WALTHAM ABBEY EN9 1XQ
TEL: 01992 702200 - Lee Valley Park Information Centre **FAX: 01992 702230**
Entrance off 'Crooked Mile' (Waltham Abbey), at junction of A121/B194. M25 Junction 26.

Peaceful gardens overlooked by the historic 12th century Abbey Church. Enjoy the summer scent of delightful Rose gardens, a sensory trail and intriguing art works. **Features:** Herbaceous borders. Rose garden. *Open: All year, daily, any reasonable time. Admission free.* **P** **Ħ** 占

EPPING FOREST   E11
DISTRICT MUSEUM,
39-41 SUN STREET,
WALTHAM ABBEY EN9 1EL
TEL: 01992 716882 FAX: 01992 700427
In centre of town, with easy access from junction 26 of the M25, and junction 7 of the M11.

Local museum, covering the social history of the Epping Forest district. Housed in Tudor and Georgian timber-framed buildings, with a small herb garden. **Features:** Herb garden. *Open: All year, Fri, Sat, Sun and Mon, 1400-1700;*

Tues, 1200-1700. Closed Wed and Thurs. Admission free. ♿ **WC** ★ 占 *(ground floor galleries and garden)*

✤ WESTCLIFF-ON-SEA   H12/13
☸ CHALKWELL PARK,
CHALKWELL AVENUE, WESTCLIFF-ON-SEA
TEL: 01702 215610 - Parks Dept,
Southend Council **FAX: 01702 215631**
From the A13, turn right into Chalkwell Avenue.

Ornamental gardens renowned for colourful bedding displays and an established Rose garden, recognised by the Royal National Rose Society. Summer 3D carpet bedding display. **Features:** Herbaceous borders and landscaped parkland. Environmental garden. Rose, wildflower and courtyard gardens. *Open: All year, daily, from 0730 (closing times subject to seasonal variations). Admission free.* **P** **WC** ☕ **Ħ** ✗ ★ 占

✤ WICKHAM BISHOPS
(nr. Witham)   H10/11

GLEN CHANTRY, ISHAMS CHASE, WICKHAM BISHOPS, NR. WITHAM CM8 3LG
TEL: 01621 891342
One and a half miles south east of Witham. Take Maldon road, then first left to Wickham Bishops. Cross narrow bridge, then turn left up track (beside 'Blue Mills').

Three acre garden planted for year round interest, with large rock gardens, ponds, shade areas, white garden and colour themed beds. Specialist perennial nursery attached. **Features:** Herbaceous borders. Rock/alpine garden. *Open: Apr to mid Oct, Fri and Sat, 1000-1600. £2/£2/50p.* ❀ **P** **WC** ☕ *(teas)*

WICKHAM PLACE FARM,   H10/11
STATION ROAD, WICKHAM BISHOPS, NR. WITHAM CM8 3JB
TEL: 01621 891282 (after 1800)
FAX: 01621 891721
From Witham, take B1018 towards Maldon. After going under A12, take third left (Station Road) to Wickham Bishops. Garden is at first house on left.

Interesting two acre walled garden, filled with huge climbers, Roses, shrubs, perennials and bulbs. Further twelve acres of natural ponds, woodland and knot gardens. **Features:** Herbaceous borders. Knot, woodland and walled gardens. *Open: Fris only, 7 Apr, 28 Apr to 28 Jul, 1 to 29 Sept, 1100-1600. Closed during Aug. £1.50/£1.50/50p (over 5yrs).* ❀ **P** **WC** ☕ **Ħ** ★ 占

84

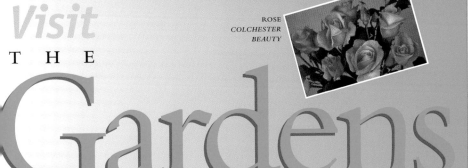

Visit THE Gardens

AT COLCHESTER

Castle park

ROSE COLCHESTER BEAUTY

HOLLY ...NGIUM

COLCHESTER'S CASTLE PARK is an oasis of horticultural splendour in the town centre. This award winning classic Victorian park is a delight for the senses all the year round. A walk through the park gives a whole variety of experiences from the stunning symmetry and colour of the formal flower beds and gardens to the picturesque tree-lined path along the River Colne.

Tranquillity reigns today but this hasn't always been so. The area around the Castle has been the location for some of the major historical events which have taken place in Colchester's long and dramatic past.

Grade II listed in the Register of Historic Parks and Gardens, Castle Park's 33 gently sloping acres (13.5ha) also provide a natural venue for a wide range of events throughout the year.

COLCHESTER

*f*OR FURTHER INFORMATION ABOUT COLCHESTER AND EVENTS IN CASTLE PARK
☞ PLEASE CALL THE COLCHESTER VISITOR INFORMATION CENTRE
1 QUEEN STREET · COLCHESTER · ESSEX · CO1 2PG · ☎ 01206 282920

✤ AYOT ST. LAWRENCE *(nr. Welwyn)* C10
SHAW'S CORNER (The National Trust),
AYOT ST. LAWRENCE,
NR. WELWYN AL6 9BX
TEL: 01438 820307
Two miles north east of Wheathamstead,
approximately two miles from B653.

The home of George Bernard Shaw from 1906 until his death in 1950. The rooms remain much as he left them, with many literary and personal effects evoking the individuality and genius of this great dramatist. The garden has richly planted borders and views over the Hertfordshire countryside. **Features:** Herbaceous borders and statuary/sculpture. Dell and fruit and vegetable gardens. *Open: 1 Apr to 29 Oct, daily (except Mon and Tues), 1300-1700. Last admission 1630 (1530 on 16,17,18 Jun and 1, 2, 21, 22, 23 Jul. Closed Good Fri, but open Bank Hol Mon. £3.50/£3.50/£1.75/£8.75 (family ticket).* 🅿 ⓦ 𝔎 ♿

✤ BENINGTON *(nr. Stevenage)* D10
BENINGTON LORDSHIP GARDENS,
BENINGTON, NR. STEVENAGE SG2 7BS
TEL: 01438 869228 FAX: 01438 869622
Take A602 from Stevenage to Hertford. Follow brown tourist signs from Watton at Stone.

Hilltop Edwardian plantsman's garden, full of surprises and interesting all year round. Castle ruins, Roses and springwater garden. **Features:** Garden folly, herbaceous borders, landscaped parkland and statuary/sculpture. Dell, fruit and vegetable, kitchen, Rose, sunken, water and wildflower gardens. Special collection of naturalised Snowdrops (Feb and Mar). *Open: Apr to Sept, Wed and Bank Hol Mon, 1200-1700. Also Sun (Apr to Aug), 1400-1700. Special openings for Snowdrops in Feb/Mar - please call (01438) 869668 £2.80/ £2.80/free.* ✤ 🅿 ⓦ 🛍 🎋 𝔎 SE - 24, 25 Jun

✤ BERKHAMSTED B11
ASHRIDGE, BERKHAMSTED HP4 1NS
TEL: 01442 843491 FAX: 01442 841209
Three miles north of Berkhamsted on the A4251 (south of the village of Little Gaddesden)

A fine garden designed by Humphry Repton and adapted by Wyatville, comprising a range of small gardens with additional features added during the Victorian period. **Features:** Arboretum, garden folly (arbour and grotto), topiary and herbaceous borders. Italian, parterre, rock/alpine, Rose, sunken and woodland gardens. 🅖 - Humphry Repton. *Open: Easter to end Sept, Sat, Sun and Bank Hols, 1400-1800. £2/£1/£1.* 🛍 🅿 ⓦ ♿

✤ CHESHUNT D11
CEDARS PARK,
THEOBALDS LANE, CHESHUNT
TEL: 01992 785555 - Borough Council offices
From North A10, past College Road lights (A121) next left off A10.

An historical park with ornamental gardens, lake, pets corner, rose walk, arboretum and tearoom. **Features:** Arboretum and landscaped parkland. Rose garden. *Open: All year, daily, 1000-dusk. Tearoom 1000-dusk (Tues-Sun, Feb-Nov). Admission free.* 🅿 ⓦ 🛍 *(seasonal only)* 🐕 ♿

✤ CHISWELL GREEN *(nr. St. Albans)* C11
🌀 THE GARDENS OF THE ROSE,
THE ROYAL NATIONAL ROSE SOCIETY,
CHISWELL GREEN,
ST. ALBANS AL2 3NR
TEL: 01727 850461 FAX: 01727 850360
Signposted from the B4630, St Albans to Watford road A414/A405 St Albans to Hatfield.

The beautiful Gardens of the Rose are a stunning spectacle from June to September, with the greatest collection of roses in the world - some 30,000 roses on display. **Features:** Iris garden, Herbaceous borders, Demonstration gardens and Cultivation trials. Rose, scent and sunken gardens. National

cont. next page

Collection of Rosa (species and cultivars).
G - Graham Stuart Thomas. *Open: Summer - 3 Jun to 24 Sept, Mon to Fri, 0900-1700; Sun and Bank Hols, 1000-1800. Summer - £4/£3.50/£2 (6-16yrs)* ♿ ❀ **P** ♿ ☂ ✗ ✗ ☂ ♿ SE - Jun-Sept

✤ **ENFIELD**

CAPEL MANOR GARDENS,   *D11/12*
BULLSMOOR LANE,
ENFIELD EN1 4RQ
TEL: 0181 366 4442 FAX: 01992 717544
Just off junction 25 of the M25.

Thirty acres of richly planted theme gardens, including Italianate maze, Japanese garden, Gardening Which?' demonstration gardens, Animal World and Victorian stables.
Features: Garden folly (temple), herbaceous borders, maze (holly), statuary/ sculpture and tropical house. Fruit and vegetable, herb, Japanese, knot, rock/alpine, Rose, scent, water, wildflower and woodland gardens. National Collections of Achillea and Sarcococca. *Open: All year, Summer 1000-1630 Mar-Oct 7 days per week. Winter 1000-1530 Nov-Feb 5 days per week. Summer £4/£3.50/£2 (3-16 yrs). Winter £3/£2/£1.* ♿ **P** ♿ ☂ ☂ ✗ ✗ ☂ ♿ SE - throughout the year, contact for details

◎ **MYDDELTON HOUSE GARDENS,** *D12*
BULLS CROSS, ENFIELD EN2 9HG
TEL: 01992 702200 FAX: 01992 650714
From junction 25 of the M25, take the A10 towards London. At the first set of traffic lights turn right, and follow the road around. The entrance to the gardens is a hidden turning on the right.

Myddelton House Gardens, created by E.A. Bowles, is a unique experience for gardeners who cherish rare and unusual plants. Attractions include thousands of naturalised bulbs, the Lunatic Asylum (home to unusual plants) and the Tulip Terrace. There is also a beautiful carp lake, conservatories and a rock garden. **Features:** Statuary/sculpture.

Rock/alpine and Rose gardens. National Collection of award winning Bearded Iris .
G - E.A. Bowles. *Open: All year, Mon-Fri (except Christmas Hols), 1000-1630. Easter to Oct, Sun, Bank Hols and NGS days, 1400-1700. £1.80/£1.20/£1.20.* ❀ **P** *(always available)* ♿ ♿ *(Sun only)* ✗ *(always available)* ♿

✤ **FRITHSDEN** *(nr. Hemel Hempstead)*   *B11*
FRITHSDEN VINEYARD, FRITHSDEN,
NR. HEMEL HEMPSTEAD HP1 3DD
TEL: 01442 864732 FAX: 01442 864732
Off the A4146, three miles from Hemel Hempstead. From Berkhamsted, follow the signs.

A three acre vineyard planted with various grape varieties, on a south-facing slope overlooking the village of Frithsden. Guided tours, winery, shop and wine-tastings.
Features: Vineyard. *Open: All year, Wed-Sat, 1000-1700; Sun, 1200-1500. Mon and Tues, by appointment only. Admission free.* ♿ **P** ♿ ✗ ☂ ♿

✤ **HADLEY WOOD** *(nr. Barnet)*   *C/D12*
THE BEALE ARBORETUM,
WEST LODGE PARK, HADLEY WOOD,
NR. BARNET EN4 0PY
TEL: 0208 2163900 FAX: 0208 2163937
Leave M25 at junction 24, take A111 south to Cockfosters. Arboretum is one mile on left.

The nearest arboretum to London, with hundreds of trees and shrubs. Opening times as below, plus two special open days with conducted tours. **Features:** Arboretum. National Collections of Elaegnus and Carpinus Betulus. *Open: Apr to Oct, Wed, 1400-1700. £1.50/£1.50/free.* **P** ♿ ♿ ✗ ✗ ☂ ♿ SE - 21 May, 29 Oct

**Edward Augustus Bowles
(1865-1954)**
Myddelton House at Enfield in Middlesex was the home of Edward A. Bowles, an enthusiastic collector, botanist and amateur gardener. His four acres of garden became a Mecca for the British gardening public with its world famous collection of rare and unusual plants. Many of the finest plants of the day were raised and distributed from here and Bowles also found time to write several popular gardening books – including 'My Garden in Spring'. After his death in 1954, the garden became overgrown and many of the unusual plants disappeared. Today, it is being restored by the Lee Valley Regional Park Authority and is home to the National Collection of award-winning Bearded Iris.

✣ HARPENDEN   C10
LW PLANTS,
23 WROXHAM WAY,
HARPENDEN AL5 4PP
TEL: 01582 768467
Off Ox Lane and Cold Harbour Lane, from B653/B652.
Compact plantsman's garden, with year-round interest. Sloping site with walls, steps, paving, large herbaceous border, Camomile lawn and alpine scree. Back garden nursery. **Features:** Herbaceous borders. Herb, rock/alpine and scent gardens. National Collection of Thymus. *Open: By appointment only, please telephone to confirm visit. Special openings for NGS on 2 Apr; 1, 29 May; 11 Jun; 16 Jul; 28 Aug and 17 Sept. £1/£1/£1.* ✿ ✗ SE - 4 Jun

✣ HATFIELD   C11
◎ HATFIELD HOUSE GARDEN,
HATFIELD HOUSE, HATFIELD AL9 5NQ
TEL: 01707 262823 FAX: 01707 275719
From M25 junction 23, head north on A1(M) for seven miles to junction 4. Follow brown signs.
A masterpiece of Jacobean garden re-creation, following the layout devised by John Tradescant. The whole forty-two acres of garden are open to connoisseurs on Fridays. **Features:** Herbaceous borders, landscaped parkland, maze (hedge), statuary/sculpture and topiary. Fruit and vegetable, herb, kitchen, knot, parterre, scent, sunken, wildflower and woodland gardens. ⑤ - John Tradescant the Elder. *Open: 25 Mar to 24 Sept, daily (except Mon), 1100-1800. Special garden 'connoisseur days' on Fri throughout season. Open on Bank Hol Mon. £6.20/£6.20/£3.10 (Fri - garden only £5.20).* ⏚ ✿ P WC ♿ � ✗ ✗ 🐕 *(not in garden)* ♿ SE - 24, 25 Jun

✣ HEMEL HEMPSTEAD   B11

◎ GADEBRIDGE PARK, LEIGHTON
BUZZARD ROAD, HEMEL HEMPSTEAD
TEL: 01442 234222 - Dacorum
Information Centre FAX: 01442 230427
Entrance to park at junction of A4146 (Leighton Buzzard road) and Queensway.
Seventy five acres of formal parkland, including seventy five metres of the River Gade. Magnificent walled garden with mixed bedding displays, and historic Charter Tower. **Features:** Landscaped parkland. Walled garden. *Open: All year, daily, any reasonable time. Admission free.* P WC ア 🐕 ♿

◎ HEMEL HEMPSTEAD WATER   B11
GARDENS, WATERHOUSE STREET,
HEMEL HEMPSTEAD
TEL: 01442 234222 - Dacorum
Information Centre FAX: 01442 230427
Located on the western side of Waterhouse Street, in the town centre.
A delightful oasis of the River Gade, with grass, shrubs and lake, home to a variety of waterbirds. Interesting pieces of artwork including Rock 'n' Roll and Platypus and Joey. *Open: All year, daily, any reasonable time. Admission free.* P (nearby) WC (nearby) 🐕 ♿

✣ HITCHIN

BARNCROFT PARK,   C9
BARNCROFT, HITCHIN
TEL: 01462 474253 FAX: 01462 474500
Attractive flower gardens with Bandstand. Facilities for bowls and tennis.
P WC

HITCHIN MUSEUM PHYSIC GARDEN, C9
PAYNES PARK, HITCHIN SG5 1EQ
TEL: 01462 434476 FAX: 01462 431316
Located beside roundabout - A505 to Luton/A602 to Stevenage/A600 to Bedford.
A small physic garden, which complements a recreation of the interior of a Victorian Chemist Shop, in the museum, which once stood in Hitchin, with plants for internal and external medicinal uses, plants used in household uses and plants used in the treatment of textiles. **Features:** Herb garden. *Open: All year, Mon-Sat, 1000-1700; Sun, 1400-1630. Admission free.* ⏚ ✿ P (limited) ✗ ♿ SE - 17- 26 May, 1-14 July

The Garden Cities of Hertfordshire
Letchworth and Welwyn Garden City in Hertfordshire, are the world's first 'Garden Cities' – a place planned to combine the benefits of both city and countryside. This was the vision of parliamentary reporter Ebenezer Howard in 1898. Trees, parks and open spaces played a major part in the design. So that control over planning could be monitored, residents would only be able to lease land. The first site chosen was Letchworth, where work began in 1903. Later, a second site was developed at Welwyn in 1919. Although neither place has followed Howard's plans completely, they have become models for the future planning of British New Towns.

✤ **KNEBWORTH** *(nr. Stevenage)* *C/D10*
◎ KNEBWORTH HOUSE, GARDENS
AND PARK, KNEBWORTH,
NR. STEVENAGE SG3 6PY
TEL: 01438 812661 FAX: 01438 811908
Direct access from junction 7 of the A1(M).

Twenty five acres of beautiful formal gardens
adjoining Knebworth House, home of the
Lytton family for over 500 years. The
elaborate gardens of the Victorian era were
simplified by Sir Edwin Lutyens. Features
include pollarded Lime avenues, Rose
garden, maze, Victorian Wilderness and
Gertrude Jekyll herb garden. **Features:**
Herbaceous borders, landscaped parkland
and maze (hedge). Herb, Rose, sunken,
water, wildflower and woodland gardens.
G - Gertrude Jekyll and Sir Edwin Lutyens.
*Open: 15 Apr-1 May daily, 6 May-21 May weekends
& Bank Hols only, 27 May-4 Jun daily, 10 Jun-2
Jul weekends only, 8 Jul-3 Sept daily, 9 Sept-1 Oct
weekends only. Closed 18 Jun. Park, gardens and
playground - £5/£5/£5 (5-16yrs). Entrance to house
(extra) - £1/50p/50p. Discounts for groups of 20+.
Garden tours available. Pre-booked tours for groups of
20+ available out of season.* ♿ ✿ P WC 🔨 *(in park
only)* ✕ 🐾 🐂 *(not in gardens)* SE - May

✤ **LETCHWORTH** *C9*
KENNEDY GARDENS,
BROADWAY, LETCHWORTH
TEL: 01462 474253 - District Council offices
Situated in the town centre.

Attractive Rose gardens, lined with Poplar
trees. *Open: All year, daily, any reasonable time.
Admission free.* P *(nearby)*

✤ **MUCH HADHAM** *E10*
THE FORGE MUSEUM AND VICTORIAN
COTTAGE GARDEN,
HIGH STREET,
MUCH HADHAM SG10 6BS
TEL: 01279 843301 FAX: 01279 843301
*A414 to Hertford - Harlow stretch, take
'The Hadhams' turning (B1004).*

Set in a beautiful village, this is a museum
about blacksmithing, with a working forge.
The Victorian Cottage Garden features a
rare early 19th century bee shelter, and a
granary. **Features:** Herbaceous borders,
fruit and vegetable, herb and rose gardens.
Herb and Rose gardens. *Open: Fri, Sat, Sun
and Bank Hol Mon, 1100-1700 (dusk in winter).
Extended opening times during temporary exhibitions.
£1/50p/50p.* ♿ ✿ P *(at village hall opposite)* WC 🔨
✕ *(if pre-booked)* 🐾 SE

✤ **RINGSHALL** *(nr. Berkhamsted)* *B10/11*
ASHRIDGE ESTATE
(The National Trust), RINGSHALL,
NR. BERKHAMSTED HP4 1LT
TEL: 01442 851227 FAX: 01442 842062
Between Northchurch and Ringshall, just off the B4506.

Magnificent and varied estate running across
the borders of Herts and Bucks, along the
main ridge of the Chiltern Hills. Woodlands,
commons and chalk downland support a rich
variety of wildlife and offer splendid walks
through outstanding scenery. Focal point is
the monument erected in 1832 to the Duke
of Bridgewater. **Features:** Arboretum.
G - Lancelot 'Capability' Brown and
Humphry Repton. *Open: All year, daily, any
reasonable time. Monument - 1 Apr to 29 Oct, Mon-
Thurs, 1400-1700. Sat, Sun and Bank Hol Mon,
1400-1730. Closed Fri, except Good Fri.
£1.20/£1.20/60p.* ♿ P WC 🔨 🐾 🐂 ♿

✤ ROYSTON   D8
PRIORY GARDENS, ROYSTON
TEL: 01462 474253 - District Council offices
Situated in the town centre.

Royston has been the best town in Anglia in Bloom twice and runner up twice in the last four years. A children's play area is included in the gardens. A sensory maze has been created in the gardens as the town's Millennium project. This is designed to be accessible to wheelchair users and those who are visually impaired. *Open: All year, daily, any reasonable time. Admission free.* 🅿 *(nearby)* 🏞

✤ ST PAUL'S WALDEN BURY   C10
ST PAUL'S WALDEN BURY GARDEN, HITCHIN SG4 8BP
TEL: 01438 871218/871229
FAX: 01438 871218
On the B651, five miles south of Hitchin.

This is the childhood home of Queen Elizabeth the Queen Mother. The 18th century landscape garden has allees and avenues covering more than 50 acres. Among them are flower and woodland gardens. **Features:** Temples, statues, amphitheatre, lake and ponds. *Open: Suns 16 Apr; 14 May; 18 Jun, 1400-1900, or £5 by appointment for both individuals and groups. £2.50/£1.25/50p* 🅿 ♿ 🐾 *(home-made teas - Sun only)* 🏞 🐕 ♿

✤ TRING   A11
◎ TRING PARK, TRING
TEL: 01442 234222 - Dacorum
Information Centre FAX: 01442 230427
Access to park via Akeman Street in Tring.

Historic 17th/18th century landscaped park, once the home of the Rothschilds. 300 acres of grass and woodland, are set on a steep slope of the Chiltern Hills, with interesting follies. **Features:** Garden folly (monument, summerhouse) and landscaped parkland. Network of walks in park. 🅶 - Charles Bridgeman and James Gibb. *Open: All year, daily, any reasonable time. Admission free.* 🅿 *(nearby)* 🏞 🐕

WARE

SCOTT'S GROTTO,   D10
SCOTTS ROAD, WARE SG12 9JQ
TEL: 01920 464131
www.scotts-grotto.org
Off the A119 (Hertford Road).

One of the finest grottos in the country, extending sixty seven feet into the hillside and decorated with flints, shells, fossils and pebbles. Please bring a torch. **Features:** Garden folly (18th century grotto and summerhouse). *Open: Apr to end Sept, Sat and Bank Hol Mon, 1400-1630. Admission free (donations welcome).* 🐕

WARE GARDEN GAZEBO'S, WARE   D10
In the centre of the town, beside the river.

Unique collection of attractive 18th century gazebos (summerhouses), belonging to houses in the High Street. Many have been recently restored, and can be viewed from the river bank. **Features:** Garden folly (gazebo) *Open: All year, daily, any reasonable time. Admission free.* 🅿 *(nearby)*

✤ WATFORD   B11/12
CHESLYN GARDENS,
NASCOTT WOOD ROAD, WATFORD
TEL: 01923 235946 FAX: 01923 232849
Take the A411 Hempstead Road (out of Watford), right up Ridge Lane, then right into Nascott Wood Road.

A three and a half acre garden, featuring woodland, herbaceous borders and a mixture of well-loved and more unusual plants. **Features:** Herbaceous borders. Rock/alpine and woodland gardens. *Open: All year, daily (except Christmas Day), dawn to dusk. Admission free.* 🅿 ♿ 🐕 ♿

Hitchin – 'Lavender Town'

Hitchin, in Hertfordshire, is known for its Lavender products which were famed world-wide. Back in 1823, the family-run company of 'Perks and Llewellyn' had ten acres of sweet-smelling fields at the end of the town's 'Lavender Way'. Sadly, the company ceased trading in 1961. Another company, 'T J Barnett', produced the Royal Hitchin Lavender water, while the firm of 'William Ransom and Son' presented Queen Victoria with Lavender water, for the Prince of Wales, when the royal trains stopped in Hitchin in 1851. The firm, which bears his name today, still produces Lavender oil.

Some of the gardens featured within these tours, have limited or restricted opening hours. We have indicated these with an *, and suggest you refer to their entry within this guide (to check opening times), before starting your journey.

GARDENS THROUGH THE CENTURIES

Jump aboard our time machine, for a journey through the history of gardens. From the medieval and Tudor delights of Stockwood, to the classical Wrest Park and eccentric Swiss Garden. **Starting point:** Luton *(Bedfordshire)* **Mileage:** 20 miles. *Morning* – explore nine centuries of garden history at Stockwood Craft Museum & Gardens. *Afternoon* - Leave Luton on the A6 north to Bedford. After about ten miles you reach the village of Silsoe. Follow the signs to Wrest Park Gardens, where you can travel through 150 years of English gardens. After your visit, return to the A6 and head north to the roundabout, where you turn right onto the A507

cont. next page

Visit Myddelton House Gardens

...and enjoy one of Enfield's best kept secrets.

Created by famous plantsman, expert botanist and author E.A. Bowles, the Gardens offer visitors something different throughout the year. In addition to the National Collection of Award Winning Bearded Iris, the Gardens also boast thousands of naturalised bulbs, a rock garden, a beautiful Carp lake and the Lunatic Asylum (home to unusual plants).

There's free car parking, and guided tours are bookable.

For more information please call: **01992 717711**

Opening Times:
Monday - Friday (except Christmas holidays) 10am - 4.30pm
Sundays & Bank Holidays, Easter - October, & National Garden Scheme Days 2pm - 5pm

Myddelton House Gardens
Bulls Cross
Enfield
Middlesex EN2 9HG

www.leevalleypark.org.uk

Lee Valley Park

Open spaces and sporting places

towards Baldock. At the second round-about, turn left onto the A600, then at the third roundabout, turn right onto the B658. Follow this for about four miles, then turn left to Old Warden. End the day at the eccentric Swiss Garden, with its grotto and tiny buildings.

UP THE GARDEN PATH
Explore the garden delights around England's oldest recorded town. Start the day at the home of Beth Chatto, then its onto the back garden of a castle, and the country estate of Marks Hall. **Starting point:** Colchester *(Essex)* **Mileage:** 14 miles *Morning* – take the A133 to Elmstead Market, and visit the 'dry and damp' Beth Chatto Gardens. Then return to Colchester to stroll in the Victorian Castle Park, and its sensory garden. *Afternoon* – leave Colchester on the A120 towards Braintree. On the bypass around the town of Coggeshall, turn right onto the B1024 towards Earls Colne. Then take the next turning on your left to the woodlands and walled garden of the Marks Hall Estate.

BLOOMIN' BEDFORDSHIRE!
On this one day tour, you can visit a tropical house full of colourful butterflies, stroll along one of England's finest river settings, and experience the record-breaking trees of Woburn Abbey. **Starting point:** Bedford *(Bedfordshire)* **Mileage:** 22 miles *Morning* – leave the town on the B660 north towards Bolnhurst. After two and half miles, turn right to the village of Wilden, to visit the tropical plants of the Bedford Butterfly Farm. Then retrace your steps to Bedford, to take a walk along the Bedford Embankment Gardens. *Afternoon* – take the A421 south to junction 13 of the M1. Here you join the A4012, following the signs to Woburn Abbey, and its 3,000 acre deer park, lakes and record-breaking trees.

FLORAL TREASURES
OF SOUTH ESSEX
Mix together Southend's colourful parks and gardens, and one of the prized patches of the Royal Horticultural Society, and you have this lovely one day tour full of floral surprises.

Starting point: Southend-on-Sea **Mileage:** 12 miles *Morning* - explore the award-winning parks and gardens of Southend-on-Sea. Established between 1900-1930 they cover over 1,000 acres. If time, then why not join one of the special 'Floral Tours'? *Afternoon* - leave Southend on the A127 towards Basildon. After about six miles, turn right onto the A130 north towards Chelmsford. Five miles later you reach the village of Rettendon. End the day amongst the Roses and Waterlillies at The Royal Horticultural Society's Garden 'Hyde Hall'.

GREAT PLANT COLLECTORS
Visit the homes and gardens connected to some of Britain's most famous collectors of plants. From E.A. Bowles at Myddelton House to stately Hatfield, haunt of John Tradescant. **Starting point:** Junction 25 of the M25 *(Hertfordshire)* **Mileage:** 20 miles *Morning* – from junction 25 of the M25, head south along the A10 towards London. At the first traffic lights, turn right and follow along the A10 towards London. At the first traffic lights, turn right and follow the road around to Myddelton House Gardens, with its rare and unusual plants. After your visit, retrace your steps back towards the A10, where on your left you will find the themed gardens of Capel Manor. *Afternoon* – return to junction 25 of the M25, and turn left. Follow the M25 to junction 23, where you head north for six miles along the A1(M), following signs to Hatfield House Garden. End the day at this Jacobean house, with its recreated 17th century gardens.

GARDENS OF THE RICH
AND FAMOUS
Mr Gibson's gardens at Saffron Walden, Lord Braybrooke's Jacobean masterpiece and the former home of 'Daisy' Countess of Warwick – explore the gardens of the rich and famous. **Starting point:** Saffron Walden (Essex) **Mileage:** 15 miles *Morning* – visit Mr Gibson's restored Bridge End Gardens. Then follow the signs to Audley End House and Gardens, and explore one of

cont. next page

the greatest Jacobean houses in England.
Afternoon – leave Saffron Walden on the
B184 south towards Great Dunmow.
After about eleven miles, turn right to
Little Easton, following signs to *The
Gardens of Easton Lodge. End the day at
the former home and gardens of 'Daisy'
Countess of Warwick.

LANDSCAPES AND GARDENS OF ROYAL HERTFORDSHIRE

From the heavenly heights of Ashridge,
discover Hemel's walled garden and
Charter Tower, Shaw's inspirational
corner and the classical childhood home
of The Queen Mother.

Starting point: Tring (Hertfordshire)
Mileage: 30 miles *Morning* – follow the
unclassified road through Aldbury, and
up onto the Ashridge Estate. At the
junction with the B4506, turn left to the
National Trust centre and enjoy a stroll
through the woodlands. Return to the
B4506 and head to Ringshall, where you
turn right to Little Gaddesden. In the
village, turn right onto a 'toll road' past
the college. Then follow the unclassified
roads through Frithsden and Potten End
to Hemel Hempstead. Explore the
walled garden at Gadebridge Park and
the nearby Water Gardens. *Afternoon* –
leave the town on the B487, and at the
roundabout with the A5183, turn left.
Then at the second roundabout, turn
right. Two miles later at the third roundabout (with the A1081), turn left. One
mile later, turn right onto the B652
(through Harpenden), then at the T-
junction with the B653, turn right. Two
miles later at the roundabout, turn left
towards Kimpton. Follow the signs to the
richly planted garden at Shaw's Corner.
When you are ready to leave, retrace
your steps back to the B651, turn right
and head to the village of *St. Paul's
Walden Bury. Visit the famous garden,
childhood home of The Queen Mother.

MAP OF
BEDFORDSHIRE, ESSEX
& HERTFORDSHIRE

MAP KEY

● **M11** Ⓢ	*Motorways*	
A74	*Dual Carriageways*	
A1066	*Primary routes*	
A144	*A or Main road*	
B1118	*B roads & Other*	
– ⓥ –	*Ferry (Vehicle)*	
	Railway	
	River	
	Lake	
	Coastline	
	Heritage coast	
	National border	
	County border	
	Urban area	
✈ Ⓗ	*Airport/Heliport*	

Please use this map only
as a guide. We advise you
consult more detailed maps
when visiting the area.

© MAPS IN MINUTES™ 1999

INDEX of Gardens